LONGEVITY IN SINGAPORE

IMPLICATIONS AND OPPORTUNITIES
for INDIVIDUALS AND SOCIETY

Helen Ko

Text © Helen Ko
© 2023 Marshall Cavendish International (Asia) Pte Ltd

Published in 2023 by Marshall Cavendish Editions
An imprint of Marshall Cavendish International

All rights reserved

No part of this publication may be reproduced, stored in a retrieval system or transmitted, in any form or by any means, electronic, mechanical, photocopying, recording or otherwise, without the prior permission of the copyright owner. Requests for permission should be addressed to the Publisher, Marshall Cavendish International (Asia) Private Limited, 1 New Industrial Road, Singapore 536196. Tel: (65) 6213 9300
E-mail: genref@sg.marshallcavendish.com Website: www.marshallcavendish.com

The publisher makes no representation or warranties with respect to the contents of this book, and specifically disclaims any implied warranties or merchantability or fitness for any particular purpose, and shall in no event be liable for any loss of profit or any other commercial damage, including but not limited to special, incidental, consequential, or other damages.

Other Marshall Cavendish Offices:
Marshall Cavendish Corporation, 800 Westchester Ave, Suite N-641, Rye Brook, NY 10573, USA • Marshall Cavendish International (Thailand) Co Ltd, 253 Asoke, 16th Floor, Sukhumvit 21 Road, Klongtoey Nua, Wattana, Bangkok 10110, Thailand • Marshall Cavendish (Malaysia) Sdn Bhd, Times Subang, Lot 46, Subang Hi-Tech Industrial Park, Batu Tiga, 40000 Shah Alam, Selangor Darul Ehsan, Malaysia

Marshall Cavendish is a registered trademark of Times Publishing Limited

National Library Board, Singapore Cataloguing-in-Publication Data
Name(s): Ko, Helen.
Title: Longevity in Singapore : implications and opportunities for individuals and society / Helen Ko.
Description: Singapore : Marshall Cavendish Editions, 2023.
Identifier(s): ISBN 978-981-4974-12-7 (paperback)
Subject(s): LCSH: Older people--Singapore. | Older people--Care--Singapore. | Older people--Services for--Singapore. | Older people--Employment--Singapore. | Aging--Singapore.
Classification: DDC 305.26095957--dc23

Printed in Singapore

To

My dearest husband, Soo Meng. Thank you for your unwavering love, care and patience always.

My beloved children, Moses (and Andrea), Noel, Judith and Matthias. It is a joy and privilege to be your mother (mother-in-law). May you utilise the manifold gifts and talents that God has blessed you with, "to do justice, and to love kindness, and to walk humbly with your God" (Micah 6:8).

My students, past and present. You have been and remain tremendous blessings to me. May you continue to employ all that you have learned to make a positive difference to the lives of seniors and their families, to our society and others in the region!

CONTENTS

Foreword — 7
Preface — 10

Part I **Background and Overview**
Chapter 1: Introduction — 14

Part II **Age-associated Changes, Disease Burden and Prevention**
Chapter 2: Physical Changes with Ageing — 26
Celestine Wee
Chapter 3: Psychological Changes with Ageing — 41
Moses Ko
Chapter 4: Medical Problems of Older Adults — 49
Moses Ko
Chapter 5: Disease Burden and Prevention — 61

Part III **Social Challenges and Integration of Seniors**
Chapter 6: Social Challenges of Population Ageing I — 70
Chapter 7: Social Challenges of Population Ageing II — 88
Chapter 8: Strategies to Promote Social Integration I — 102
Chapter 9: Strategies to Promote Social Integration II — 108

Part IV	**Harnessing the Potential of Seniors**	
Chapter 10:	Seniors' Employment and Financial Security	124
Chapter 11:	Harnessing the Potential of an Ageing Workforce	136
Chapter 12:	Lifelong Learning	145

Part V	**Recommendations and Conclusion**	
Chapter 13:	Recommendations for Public Policies	159
Chapter 14:	Moving Forward	173

Appendix: Community Resources (Selected)	177
References	183
Contributors	203
Acknowledgements	205
About the Author	207

Foreword

When I regarded the title of this book and surveyed the chapter headings therein, I wondered to myself, "Who is this book intended for?", "Who will it benefit?" and "What does a longer life span mean for each one of us and for our society?"

Longevity is sought after by everyone generally. In many cultures, it is good to have a long life, it is considered a blessing. In some cases, it is taken as evidence of a life well-lived thus far. Modern living conditions and advances in medicine have enabled us to live longer, constituting part of the reason why we are contemplating an ageing population with hope and yet with some concern.

Living longer is one thing, living longer contentedly, meaningfully, happily, with dignity and accepted well by the rest of the community is another. These expectations of longevity are a wonderful outcome to have, but which require much determination and effort to attain. Greying well is not a challenge for the aged to overcome alone – the community in which the elderly live and function is part of the solution and which will bear the outcomes of how issues of an ageing population are dealt with. Longevity presents challenges of a multi-faceted, multi-dimensional nature, and thus necessitates an inter-disciplinary approach. It engenders a whole-of-community involvement.

I am into that phase of life one would class as 'elderly', and I know I have concerns about what I will be facing in my future years. I can plan some, but I will need support and guidance on how I should go about dealing with a future I have not thought much about in my younger days. Which brings me to the questions I have articulated earlier.

Those who will live longer, well-past 'retirement' age should be aware of all the changes that will occur – physiologically, mentally, emotionally, psychologically, financially, relationally, and so on – and be prepared to face and cope well with the imminent changes, and continue living with purpose. Those coming behind in age should also begin to know what to expect, including the young. This will heighten their awareness of their own future condition and preparedness to cope, as well as develop an ability to understand seniors and accommodate their needs. Society as a whole must develop acceptance of more seniors in its midst; all should be advocates of the welfare of the aged as all will head towards being elderly if longevity in life is bestowed. Infrastructure and social care will need to match the needs of the elderly. When longevity is accompanied by ill-health and dissatisfaction or dis-orientation with life, policies, programmes and services to provide alleviation and support will be critical.

But it is important to note that older adults are a very heterogeneous group, in terms of their functional and cognitive abilities, capacities, preferences, life experiences, etc. Therefore, they need to be listened to, and policies and interventions should take their perspectives into account. If this is done, and planning and management for longer living is carried out in an informed way through research, practice and ground engagement, there can be continued opportunities for personal growth and contentment of our seniors, and greater social integration of the elderly into society. Moreover, valuable human resource can be tapped by the economy and society. All of these will lead to the maturing of a caring and inclusive society.

In the end, the benefits will accrue to all who live in that kind of society.

Professor Cheong Hee Kiat
Immediate Past President
Singapore University of Social Sciences

Preface

By 2030, one in four Singaporeans will be aged 65 or older. The impact of population ageing will pervade all levels and arenas of Singapore society.

At the individual and familial levels, age-associated changes and illnesses will exert increasing demand for more and better healthcare, eldercare, and social and community support services.

At the organisational level, the effects of an ageing workforce will require adaptations in work processes, systems, policies and practices to maintain efficiency and productivity of older workers for business sustainability.

At the societal level, health and healthcare, social care and delivery, employment and employability of older adults for financial security in retirement reflect the need for appropriate elder-friendly infrastructures such as barrier-free accessibility features in transport and housing, as well as effective, timely and targeted public policies.

The costs to finance population ageing are key concerns for the Singapore government. Some people have suggested that there could be a heavier financial burden on the working population due to the need to raise taxes arising from the above changes as the population ages. It was further argued that intergenerational discord or tensions may arise as the burden on the younger working population to support the older age groups will increase with time. It has, therefore, been a key concern of the Singapore government to address the impact, implications and challenges arising from this demographic transition in Singapore.

Against the above backdrop, the aims of this book are as follows.

Firstly, it seeks to engender in readers a better understanding of age-associated physical and psychological changes and diseases, including the attendant costs and implications to society. The impact on the healthcare systems, healthcare costs, manpower and care delivery are also discussed.

Secondly, it highlights the social care and integration challenges of population ageing, and the spectrum of infrastructural, social and other supports/tools required and/or available to facilitate seniors to age in their familiar environment within the community, that is, to "age-in-place". Support and training for family and professional caregivers for more effective care delivery to seniors are also elaborated. These are crucial to prevent the marginalisation of seniors and foster a more socially inclusive society.

Thirdly, issues and challenges associated with an ageing workforce such as productivity, technological advancement, digitalisation, ageism, multi-generational workplaces, extending working lifespan, and harnessing the potential and the retirement adequacy of seniors are explained. This book emphasises the necessity and benefits of integrating older workers fully into their workplaces, as well as the necessary changes in organisational policies and practices to achieve this goal.

Finally, contrary to the often grim and negative portrayal of the impact of population ageing on society, for example, the "Silver Tsunami", this book emphasises the vast opportunities and dividends that could result from longevity in the 21st century, premised on the fulfilment of several key caveats.

To align with the above aims, this book is organised into five parts. However, it should be noted that whilst this book is organised into these parts for the purpose of presentation and to enhance clarity, in real-life context, the issues and challenges of an ageing population are intertwined, multifaceted, multi-layered and complex. It therefore requires the concerted efforts of all relevant stakeholders to work towards the desired aims.

Ultimately, the hope and goal of this book is that older adults will be able to age gracefully in Singapore, living out their golden years with dignity in the community, and be accorded the opportunities to continue to contribute meaningfully to society and live purposeful lives.

Part I

Background and Overview

Chapter 1

Introduction

"The true measure of any society can be found in how it treats its most vulnerable members."
Mahatma Gandhi

Population Ageing: Current Global Trends
Global population ageing is currently one of the most significant and urgent medical and socio-economic issues worldwide. With falling fertility rates and remarkable increases in life expectancies globally, the pace of population ageing will continue to accelerate. The World Health Organisation (WHO) projects the number of persons aged 65 or older will grow from an estimated 524 million in 2010 to nearly 1.5 billion in 2050, with most of the increase in developing countries (United Nations [UN], 2019).

With fewer children born and people living longer, older adults constitute an increasing proportion of the total population. In many developed countries, fertility rates have fallen below the replacement rate of two live births per woman. Japan, Finland and Italy are currently ranked the countries with the oldest populations (Rudnicka et al., 2020). Amongst the Organization for Economic Co-operation and Development (OECD) countries, Greece, Korea, Poland, Portugal, Slovenia and Spain are classified as the fastest ageing countries. Hence, the WHO has recognised that population ageing is a global phenomenon and is addressing this issue as a priority. Countries need to maximise the benefits and manage the risks associated with population ageing. The UN has set up a global collaboration named *Decade of Healthy Ageing (2021–2030)*. Its purpose is to bring together and align goals amongst governments, civil society, international agencies, professionals, academia, the media and the private sector to improve the lives of older persons, their families and the communities in which they live (Rudnicka et al., 2020).

The 2019 World Population Ageing trends revealed an increase in the number of individuals living beyond 65 years around the world (UN, 2019). Globally, a person aged 65 years in 2015–2020 could expect to live, on average, an additional 17 years. By 2045–2050, that figure will increase to 19 years. Life expectancy beyond age 65 is projected to increase in all countries. Women currently outlive men by 4.8 years (UN, 2019).

Population ageing will continue to put increased financial pressure on old-age support systems. In countries such as the United Kingdom and in Latin America, where the Government provides healthcare for the general population, ageing will increase the fiscal pressure on the country's revenue, particularly if taxation patterns remain unchanged. In countries where healthcare costs are borne by the individual and family, such as those in Southeast Asia, older adults and their families are likely to experience greater pressure to finance their consumption during old age. There is a greater recognition to formulate and implement social policies that can be sustained over the long term to alleviate poverty, reduce inequality, enhance social cohesion and promote social inclusion of older adults.

In 2016, the WHO proposed a *Global Strategy and Action Plan for Ageing and Health for 2016–2020*. Five strategic objectives to enable a world in which every individual has the opportunity to live a long and healthy life were identified. The first objective was a commitment to take action on healthy ageing in every country. The second goal was to create and develop environments that would be friendly to older people, such as age-friendly infrastructure and communities. The third goal was to align all healthcare systems to meet the needs of older people. This is to meet the complex and chronic medical needs of older adults seeking healthcare. The fourth objective was to create reliable and appropriate systems for providing long-term care in the home, community and institutions. The last goal was to improve effective methods in monitoring and studying the issue of healthy ageing. This *Global Strategy and Action Plan* was adopted by WHO's 194-member states, including Singapore (Rudnicka et al., 2020).

Singapore's Ageing Population: Impact and Implications
Consistent with global trends, Singapore faces the challenges of a rapidly ageing population. This is attributed to increasing life expectancies and prolonged low and declining fertility rates. The average life expectancy in Singapore is 83.9 years (Singapore. Department of Statistics, 2021b). Men live an average of 81.5 years. Women outlive them by almost five years at 86.1 years. The proportion of citizens aged 65 and older has increased from 10.1 per cent in 2010 to 16.8 per cent in 2020. This figure is expected to increase to 23.7 per cent in 2030. By 2030, one in four Singaporeans would be aged 65 or older (Singapore. Department of Statistics, 2021b).

The compounding effects of falling fertility rates and increasing life expectancies also result in fewer children available to provide care for their ageing parents. The old-age support ratio has been declining since the 1970s. The Population 2020 Census reported that the old-age support ratio of residents, computed as the ratio of residents aged 20–64 years for each resident aged 65 years and over, declined from 10.5 in 1990 to 4.0 in 2021 (Singapore. Department of Statistics, 2021a). The old-age support ratio refers to the ratio of the population who may be economically productive to the number of older people who may be dependent on others for support. This is a trend of concern as it implies there are now fewer working adults supporting older persons in Singapore.

Therefore, since the early 1980s, the Singapore government has set up various high-level inter-ministerial committees and councils to address the ramifications of population ageing. These included the Committee on the Problems of the Aged (1982), chaired by then Minister of Health, Mr Howe Yoon Chong; the Advisory Council on the Aged (1989), chaired by then Minister of Law, Professor Shunmugam Jayakumar; and followed by several others. Members of all the committees and councils comprised ministers from various ministries, as well as industry experts. The latest committee was the Ministerial Committee on Ageing, chaired by Singapore's former Health Minister, Mr Gan Kim Yong. It was established to coordinate government policies and programmes related to population ageing. The Committee launched an *Action Plan for Successful Ageing* (Ministry of Health [MOH], 2016a) in 2015. This plan forms the nation's blueprint for preparing Singaporeans to age well. The plan will be refreshed in 2022.

The impact and implications of population ageing pervades all levels and arenas of Singapore society. The ensuing section discusses these in greater detail.

At an Individual Level

Based on a report released by the Ministry of Health, it was found that as average life expectancy increases, more Singaporeans are spending more years in poor health resulting from heart diseases, stroke, cancer, diabetes and mental illnesses (MOH, 2019). In the 2019 National Population Health Survey, the proportion of Singapore residents with self-reported chronic diseases continued to increase (MOH, 2020). Multiple chronic conditions and co-morbidities (one or more additional conditions often co-occurring with a primary condition) affect the majority of seniors, with one in 15 Singaporeans reporting to suffer from diabetes; one in six suffer from hypertension and one in seven suffer from hyperlipidaemia. As with increasing age, the proportion of older adults requiring assistance in their activities of daily living (ADL), such as feeding, grooming and toileting, also increases. With increasing trends in disability burden, there will be more older adults who require physical assistance and more care hours by caregivers.

The compounding effects of falling fertility rates and increasing life expectancies could result in fewer children looking after their ageing parents/parents-in-law, who have care needs due to declining health as they age. Hence, in recent years, the viability of the family as the main care provider for older adults has been called into question.

Seniors who lose the ability to carry out their ADL such as showering, feeding themselves or the ability to ambulate or walk, may feel their sense of self-worth and dignity being challenged (Singh & Misra, 2009). They may view themselves as burdens to their families and may thus seek ways to reduce their families' burdens. Such mindsets could manifest in dire social phenomena such as geriatric depression or elder suicide. In the latest figures published by the Samaritans of Singapore (SOS), it was reported that of the 452 suicides committed in 2020,

154 of them were by persons aged 60 or older. Noteworthily, while the number of cases in this category has risen, the number of calls for help received by SOS from this group has decreased compared to 2019, suggesting that although seniors experience distress, they are not coming forward to seek help. This phenomenon is even more concerning if we note the link between age and suicide rates. To illustrate, in Singapore, there were 8.91 suicides per 100,000 for all ages in 2017. The figure rose to 24.06 per 100,000 for those aged 70 or older in the same year (Ko, 2021a).

For seniors, another impact of ageing is social isolation. For most of them, family members form their closest social ties and whom they would first turn to for help and assistance. However, as family size shrinks, many seniors are living alone. Moreover, as their siblings, friends and peers pass on, the problem of social isolation and experience of loneliness are aggravated. Such social phenomena are a growing concern as Singapore's population ages.

At a Familial Level

One of the key pillars of Singapore's national ideology is that "families are the building blocks of society". The traditional espoused belief is that the provision of care for the elderly is the responsibility of the family. However, in the recent decade, the family care system has come under tremendous pressure due to changing demographics and other social factors.

The changing demographics has resulted in a "sandwich generation" whereby working adults are required to provide physical care as well as financial support for both the young and the old. Research released by NTUC Income reported that only one-fifth of young people in Singapore believed their parents have enough personal savings to finance their retirement. Of those surveyed, only 15 per cent trusted that their parents have planned for retirement, such that they need not worry about providing for them (Mui, 2018). However, it was reported that only eight per cent of young people today were confident of having enough savings to financially support their retired parents. The same study found that 70 per cent believed they would need to downgrade their lifestyle in order to care for their parents and 47 per cent were not financially ready to provide for their parents in the event of unforeseen events (Poh, 2019). Although the survey revealed that filial values are still ingrained in modern Singapore, mounting challenges experienced by three-generational families are evident. These include increased financial expenses such as paying for children's education, as well as supporting elderly parents' medical costs.

The rising costs of living in modern Singapore often results in women having to fulfil the roles of both working adults and caregivers at home simultaneously. In *The Survey on Informal Caregiving* (Chan et al., 2012), it was noted there were more female caregivers compared to males. Women were found to be the main contributors of caregiving duties for their elderly parents/parents-in-laws. Female caregivers were also more likely to report negative health outcomes as a result of caregiving duties. In a qualitative study by Mehta & Thang (2017), adult children caregivers often expressed mounting physical, emotional, psychological and financial stress from caregiving duties.

Elder abuse may also be a consequence of caregiving strain. In Singapore, cases of elder abuse have been on the rise. Specialists working in care centres focusing on family violence noted that often older adults, "especially the non-active, frail or vulnerable ones" who are not known to the community, are at risk of elder abuse (Tan, 2020).

In addition, with increasing globalisation and temporary migration for work, adult children may not be available to meet the physical care needs of older adults. The duty of providing support and care needs may then fall on the shoulders of foreign domestic workers. Issues such as neglect and abuse also may result from caregiving strain experienced by these domestic workers who are providing care for seniors. This raises another issue of the competencies required of these workers to provide quality or adequate care for their elderly charges.

As elder abuse cases are often under-detected and under-reported, and as the number of older adults increases exponentially in Singapore, it is imperative to address this issue of protecting the vulnerable older adults.

At the Organisational and Societal Levels
At the organisational and societal levels, with the shrinking of the working-age population, there have been concerns raised regarding the sustainability of Singapore's economic growth and whether productivity can be maintained. The need for Singapore to adapt to an ageing workforce is inevitable. With higher life expectancies, many seniors in Singapore recognise that their savings in the Central Provident Fund (CPF) are inadequate to finance their retirement. In the *National Survey of Senior Citizens 2011*, the majority of respondents who were employed or returning to work cited money as the reason for the need for continual employment (Kang et al., 2013). It was obvious that money remained a critical consideration in the decision to continue or seek employment amongst older adults in Singapore. Singapore's philosophy of self-reliance and personal responsibility (or familial responsibility), where financial support at a subsistence level will only be given by the State as a last resort, is still rather deeply entrenched in our society, particularly amongst the older adults.

A challenge of employers in managing an ageing workforce is the necessity of integrating and even optimising the experience and abilities of older workers in the context of diverse, multi-ethnic, multinational and multi-generational workplaces. This may pose a challenge if ageist attitudes persist and continue to work against seniors in employment. There are also concerns regarding older workers' ability to cope with rapidly evolving technologies and maintain productivity in a highly competitive and globalised labour market.

At a societal level, population ageing is likely to pose a greater burden on public finance. Seniors who are unable to work and those in the lower income groups who are unable to support themselves or lack support from family members would require various forms of assistance from the community and the State. Moreover, the necessity of expanding intermediate and long-term care facilities to cater for the needs of seniors, including those without family support, is imperative.

Currently, Singapore mitigates the impact of an ageing population and workforce through immigration. However, this strategy of immigration is not without its challenges: socially, politically, culturally, *etc*. Moreover, there are several social trends, such as the rising number of unmarried adults, an increase in the proportion of the elderly living alone or as couples, the rise in divorce rates and the unmet needs of family caregivers. Against such a dynamic environment, policy-makers would need to regularly re-evaluate if existing social policies are still relevant and adequate in addressing these evolving developments.

Despite the above challenges, there is a growing acknowledgement of the positive effects of an ageing population. For example, the number of older adults volunteering in the community is increasing. A survey conducted by the National Volunteer and Philanthropy Centre revealed that the rate of volunteerism among older adults doubled from 2008 to 2016 (Ministry of Culture, Community and Youth, 2019). Older volunteers spend longer hours volunteering and are more committed to their roles as volunteers. Older adults see themselves as change agents who can impact and give back to society. It is therefore important to recognise their contributions through their roles, for example, as grassroots leaders, silver generation ambassadors and befrienders to socially isolated seniors in the community.

There are also positive advantages of an ageing workforce. Older workers often possess many years of experience in their jobs and workplaces. With experience comes invaluable tacit competencies and institutional knowledge (Bersin & Chamorro-Premuzic, 2019). Older workers are often more composed, confident and require less supervision. Older employees, in general, also tend to display a greater level of professionalism. They are more likely to be punctual and fully focused on their work, while being less open to distractions such as social media. All these, in turn, translate to more time-efficiency and would also be cost-effective for their companies. On the other hand, younger workers, often at the beginning of their careers, are more interested to look out for better salaries and higher positions, and are generally more susceptible to changing jobs. This is usually not the case with older workers, who appreciate stability and tend to remain longer in a company. Lastly, a very important and useful role that older workers can fill is related to succession planning, by being mentors to younger colleagues. Their ability to impart knowledge and skills to those with less experience in the company would not only benefit the organisation but would also boost the country's economic growth (International Labour Organization [ILO], 2019). The above findings on the positive aspects of an ageing workforce are in line with my own extensive experience in conducting training programmes for companies and counselling of seniors.

Against the above backdrop, the following chapters will discuss and elaborate in considerable detail the implications, challenges and opportunities of population ageing, and also propose a suite of strategies to address them within the Singapore context.

Part II

Age-associated Changes, Disease Burden and Prevention

Chapter 2

Physical Changes with Ageing

Celestine Wee

"Even to your old age and grey hairs I am He, I am He who will sustain you. I have made you and I will carry you; I will sustain you and I will rescue you."
Isaiah 46:4, *The Bible*

Growing old is a normal and natural process and should not be seen as a disease process. Besides chronological ageing based on calendar age, individuals age biologically, psychologically, sociologically and spiritually. However, chronological age is not an accurate predictor of a person's physical health status. There is increased recognition worldwide to differentiate "normal ageing" from disease or pathological changes. Many of the physical changes previously attributed to ageing have now been debunked to be more likely caused by lifestyle variables. For example, aches and pains usually attributed to ageing are more likely due to sedentary lifestyles rather than ageing *per se*. The ageing process is irreversible and physical decline usually occurs gradually over time, except when illness strikes.

It is important to recognise that ageing is a highly diverse process. Some individuals age faster than others. There is an enormous variation in the rate of the ageing process among individuals of the same chronological age (Franceschi et al., 2018). Some individuals may age faster than others depending on their genetic make-up, lifestyle and the environment they live in. For example, an older person who has always been physically active may exhibit physiological functions of someone much younger than him, and *vice versa*. This is referred to as inter-individual variations in the ageing process. Such was the case of 100-year-old Fauja Singh, who became the oldest runner to complete a marathon in Toronto. There is also intra-individual variation to the ageing process. This refers to the differential rates at which the different physical systems in a person age (Franceschi et al., 2018). For instance, a young person may have a failing liver but a healthy heart.

Although ageing is not synonymous with disease, older adults in general are more susceptible to disease than the young. Loss of body reserves due to physiological changes brought about by the ageing process increases the elderly person's vulnerability to illness.

Physiological changes due to ageing can be classified under the following domains:
- sensory (vision, hearing, taste, smell);
- integumentary (skin);
- cardiovascular (heart, lungs, blood vessels);
- haematological (blood) and the immune system;
- gastrointestinal (gut);
- urinary and renal (kidneys);
- endocrine (hormones);
- nervous system (nerves, spinal cord, brain); and
- musculoskeletal system (bones, joints, muscles, ligaments).

Sensory

Age-related changes to the sensory system are classified under visual, hearing, taste and smell.

Visual

Many older adults suffer from visual impairment. Poor vision in older adults has been found to be associated with increased falls and accidents, increased dependency on caregivers. There is also an increased prevalence of depression in older adults with visual impairment. The most common age-associated visual change is presbyopia, also known commonly as "lao hua", which usually occurs after the age of 40 due to the loss of lens elasticity. This results in a failure of near vision and the older adult compensates by moving reading material further away in order to get a good focus. This may be possible in early stages but becomes ineffective as the print becomes smaller from a further reading distance. This problem can be rectified by using a pair of reading glasses or if reading from a computer, by increasing the font size. Without such measures, the older person would have greater difficulty in reading or performing tasks that require visual focus at a short distance.

As we age, due to the thickening and clouding of the eye lenses, we may develop cataracts. This can result in lower visual acuity, as well as the loss of perception of distance and depth. Dense and thick cataracts can interfere with daily activities of living such as bathing and toileting. It may increase the risk of falls for the older adult whose visual acuity is severely decreased due to cataracts. Nevertheless, cataracts can be treated surgically and implantation of an intraocular lens during surgery can restore good central and peripheral vision for the elderly.

Another eye condition that commonly affects older adults is glaucoma. This is a painful eye condition due to increased intraocular pressure in the eye. The increase in pressure can lead to damage in the retina and optic nerve and may result in blindness if left untreated. Age-related macular degeneration (AMD) is also another leading cause of blindness in seniors. In AMD, macula cells start to atrophy leading to progressive loss of central vision. Older adults with diabetes would also commonly have an eye condition, known as diabetic retinopathy. This is usually caused by poor diabetes control and in advanced stages may even lead to visual loss and blindness.

Other visual changes which occur with ageing include:
1. Increased glare, making driving at night difficult and even potentially dangerous for the older adult.
2. Poor colour discrimination, which increases the tendency to mistake one colour for another. This can result in the selection of wrong daily items or even medications.
3. Difficulty in adapting to dark surroundings, which poses a greater risk of falling when walking from a brightly lit environment to dim surroundings.
4. Dry eyes due to decrease in tear production which may result in eye irritation, blurred vision and occasional eye redness. This can be easily treated by using eye lubricants frequently.

Hearing

With ageing, degeneration within the inner ear and along the nerve pathways to the brain may impact hearing. In addition, it can also result in a decreased ability to balance, as well as an increased risk of falling due to ageing changes to the vestibular system. Most older adults complain of difficulty in hearing, especially when there are loud background noises. Seniors also express difficulty in hearing high-pitched sounds. Approximately one-third of older adults from age 65 to 75 and half of those aged 75 and above have age-related hearing loss known as presbycusis. More men than women are affected by hearing loss.

Hearing loss interferes with communication. As a result of hearing loss, the elderly person may conclude that others are not speaking clearly when in reality the problem is faulty consonant perception. This could result in unnecessary misunderstandings and interpersonal conflicts or social withdrawal. Although the use of hearing aids can greatly alleviate the problem of hearing loss, some elderly persons are either too embarrassed to put them on or they are unable to adapt to using them.

> Tips to recognise hearing loss in the elderly:
> 1. Difficulty hearing over the telephone.
> 2. Trouble following a conversation when two or more persons are speaking at the same time.
> 3. Others complaining that the senior sets the TV volume too loud.
> 4. Having to strain to understand conversations.
> 5. Unable to hear due to background noises.
> 6. Having a sense that others seem to be mumbling.
> 7. Having a problem understanding women and children talking.

Taste and Smell

Older persons may notice a decrease in the sense of taste at around age 60. There is a decrease in the number of taste buds resulting in decreased flavour detection. Many older adults tend to complain of food tasting bland and may add more salt and flavouring to their food in order to enhance the taste – a practice which may not be helpful for certain medical conditions like hypertension, which calls for a low-salt diet. Intergenerational conflicts may also arise as a result, when the older person uses more salt in cooking. Other common oral conditions that arise from ageing include dry mouth (xerostomia) because of a reduction in saliva, which is often a side effect of consumption of chronic medications.

As we age, reduction in olfactory receptors can reduce odour detection. Changes occurring in the sense of smell have behavioural implications for the proper ingestion of food, for safety and even concerns for personal hygiene. The older adult may not be able to detect gas leakages, which could be fatal. Those with reduced olfactory perception may not be aware of body odours or other aspects of personal hygiene. This can in turn be offensive to those around them.

Integumentary (Skin)
The skin is the largest, most visible human organ, measuring up to two square metres in an average adult human body. As we age, our skin is more susceptible to dryness due to age-related dermal changes. This is the result of thinning of the epidermal layer and reduced cell turnover rate. The dermis loses about 20 per cent of its thickness when we age, resulting in a paper-thin and transparent appearance. The ageing skin also loses its elasticity with the decrease in collagen and elastin production. Hence, skin folds, especially around the face, become more prominent. Skin tears are also more common in the older adult as the skin becomes more fragile. Thus, they are more prone to trauma and pressure sores especially among bony prominences. When prolonged pressure is exerted on the tissues, there is a lack of blood supply to these tissues. The tissues are then deprived of oxygen and nutrients, resulting in dead tissue, also known as tissue necrosis. Certain chronic diseases also predispose the older adult to pressure ulcers. These includes diabetes, spinal cord injuries, fractures and arthritis.

Pigment producing cells called melanocytes diminish with ageing, resulting in greying of the hair. In addition, hair follicles become sparse and the hair has a finer and more brittle texture. In cold weather, such hair has poor insulating ability and the older adult would not be able to tolerate cold temperatures well.

As older adults age, they are also more susceptible to skin disorders such as senile purpura (formation of purple bruises following minor trauma), psoriasis (red, itchy, scaly patches on elbows, trunk and scalp), skin tags (small, soft, skin-coloured growths on the skin) and herpes zoster, also known as shingles. Skin disorders can be painful for older adults as they age. It may also trigger feelings of shame and low self-esteem due to significant changes in their appearance. This is an important point to consider as such conditions may force the older adult into social isolation.

Although there is a relatively lower incidence of nonmelanoma skin cancers in the Asian population compared to Caucasians, the numbers have been increasing over the past three decades. As older adults undergo more changes to their skin as they age, they should have a monthly self-assessment of their skin to detect any early signs of skin cancer. The ABCD method is a useful tool which comprises of checking if a lesion or mole has:

1. an Asymmetrical shape;
2. irregular Borders;
3. uneven Colour; or
4. a change in Diameter.

While it may be commonly observed that older adults have rough, scaly and cracked skin, we should not dismiss it as a normal part of ageing. The skin thickens and roughens following years of cumulative exposure to and damage from the sun (solar keratosis). There are good general skincare measures that seniors can undertake to manage underlying skin issues:

- Use mild, pH-balanced skin wash. Avoid alcohol-based products that will dry the skin.
- Avoid hot baths as they will strip away the natural oils produced by the skin.
- Dry thoroughly in between skin folds after showering.
- Hydrate the skin twice daily using skin creams or fragrance-free moisturisers.
- When in the sun, wear sunscreen that blocks UVA and UVB rays with SPF 30 or higher.
- Eat a well-balanced diet and optimise nutrition for those at risk of pressure ulcers.
- Attend yearly diabetic foot screening for those with diabetes.

Cardiovascular System

The top two global causes of mortality in the elderly population based on the latest statistics from the WHO are cardiovascular diseases, namely ischaemic heart disease and stroke. Ischaemic heart disease and stroke together accounted for a global "15.2 million deaths in 2016". Based on death statistics published by the Ministry of Health (MOH), ischaemic heart disease was ranked the third leading cause of death in Singapore (MOH, 2022). Arteriosclerosis, hardening of the arteries, is the most common disease of the arteries affecting the elderly population. It is widely considered to be an inevitable consequence of the natural ageing process. It involves a loss of elastic fibres as well as increased calcium deposits, leading to a thickening of the walls of the arteries. Atherosclerosis is the most prevalent type of arteriosclerosis with the progressive build-up of fatty tissues and plaque within the arterial walls, and it is the leading factor responsible for cardiovascular disease in older adults. This includes hypertension, heart attacks and strokes. Atherosclerosis is often found in the aorta (major blood vessels arising from the heart and supplying blood to the rest of the body) and the coronary arteries (vessels supplying blood to the heart muscles). Risk factors of cardiovascular diseases include both non-modifiable risk factors such as age, gender and ethnicity, as well as modifiable risk factors. Modifiable health risk factors (MHRFs) include smoking, diet, obesity and exercise. Changes in lifestyles of older persons can reduce the risk of developing cardiovascular diseases. Interventions targetted at MHRFs can significantly reduce the morbidity and mortality rates among these older adults.

Respiratory System

Respiratory efficiency does decrease with age. Age-related changes include progressive costal cartilage calcification, resulting in a stiffer ribcage. This would lead to the weakening of respiratory muscles, hence decreasing respiratory function. Fibrosis and atrophy of alveoli or air sacs in the lungs decreases the surface area for gas exchange. This translates to less stamina for the older adult to participate in prolonged physical activities. Presbylaryngis refers to the changes in voice pitch caused by the thinning or ageing of the vocal cords. This results in a higher, reedy voice that is difficult for a listener to hear and requires more effort from the older adult to speak to be heard.

Hematological (Blood) System

Age-related changes to the immune system is referred to as immunosenescence and results in a decrease in immune functioning. The older person may be more vulnerable to infections and diseases due to a decrease in the supply of new T cells, a type of white blood cells important in the body's defence against infection. In addition, there is also some decline in T-cell function. As a result, common infections would be more severe for the older person, with slower recovery and reduced chances of developing adequate immunity after being infected. In today's context of a COVID-19 pandemic, older adults aged 65 and above are reported to have increased risk of severe illness, requiring hospitalisation in intensive care units, oxygen support and ventilator care. Immunosenescence and chronic inflammatory body responses were the major drivers of the high mortality rates in older patients infected with COVID-19.

The competency of the older adult's immune system is also dependent on nutrition and lifestyle variables. When working with older adults, there should be an emphasis on how to support their immune system. This includes a diet adequate in iron and vitamins, reduced fat intake and avoiding a sedentary lifestyle.

Gastrointestinal System

The process of digestion slows down with age and there may be reduced efficiency in gastric emptying, but marked changes are uncommon. The gastrointestinal systems of most older adults remain adequate to meet nutritional demands. However, with ageing, there is a decrease in liver weight, reduced liver blood flow and liver function, which can result in impaired drug clearance. As most medications taken are cleared by the liver, this could lead to an increased risk of drug-drug interaction and adverse drug reaction. Therefore, in general, most doctors when prescribing medications to the elderly will start with low dosages.

Another common complaint among older adults is the problem of constipation. Constipation is defined as the difficulty in passing hard, dry stools or a decrease in frequency of elimination. Factors contributing to constipation include slower intestinal mobility due to ageing, too little fibre in the diet, reduced diet and fluid intake due to diseases or difficulty in swallowing and lack of physical activity. Introducing good

general measures in educating older adults can help with avoiding constipation and includes the following:
- Drink plenty of fluids, at least eight glasses of water a day.
- Eat more high-fibre food like fruits, vegetables, cereal, oatmeal and wholemeal products.
- Exercise regularly, three to five times a week, for at least 30 minutes each time.
- Have regular bowel habits, for example, after breakfast when one's intestinal activity is usually very active.
- If constipation persists, to seek medical evaluation. This is especially important if there is presence of blood in stools and signs of weight loss.

Urinary and Renal System

There are anatomical changes to the kidneys as an individual ages, and these may result in gradual reduced efficiency of the urinary system. The slight decrease in kidney length and the greater reduction in renal blood flow can reduce the kidneys' ability to remove drugs. This may increase the potential risk of drug toxicity. Lessened bladder capacity, weaker bladder muscle tone and increased contractions due to ageing can lead to frequent and more urgent urination in older adults. In addition, the need to urinate may be delayed until the bladder is full, hence resulting in possible incontinence. The pattern of urine excretion alters, with a higher volume of urine passed at night compared to daytime. This further contributes to sleep disturbances for the older adult during the night. An increased incidence of urinary tract infections (UTIs) occurs with age, affecting more women than men. Women are more likely to develop UTI due to a shorter urethra and its anatomical proximity to the rectum, leading to possible bacterial contamination of the urinary tract. Reduced bladder emptying and enlarged prostates in men can also increase the risk of UTIs.

Endocrine System

There is a reduction in the gland size and secretion of hormones with age. However, due to the complexity of the endocrine system, it is difficult to ascertain the effects of ageing on specific endocrine glands. Pancreatic secretions decrease with age. One significant condition affecting older adults is Type 2 diabetes. Type 2 diabetes is characterised by high blood sugar levels resulting from insulin resistance, where one's body cells do not respond normally to insulin, resulting in a high blood glucose level in the body. Insulin is a hormone made by the pancreas that "acts like a key" to let blood sugar into the cells of the body to be used for energy. High blood sugar also decreases the elasticity of blood vessels and causes them to narrow. This can lead to a reduced supply of blood and oxygen in blood vessels, resulting in high blood pressure and damage to large and small blood vessels. Large vessel disease affecting the heart and blood vessels include heart attacks and stroke. Damage to small vessels in the eyes, kidneys and nerves can occur too, leading to diabetic retinopathy, chronic renal failure and diabetic foot ulcers. By 2030, the number of Singapore residents above age 40 with diabetes is projected to increase to 600,000, from about 400,000 in 2016 (SingHealth, n.d.).

In 2016, the MOH declared a "War on Diabetes", to rally the entire nation to tackle diabetes. It was estimated that the healthcare cost to the nation was approximately over $1 billion a year to manage diabetes. Then Minister of Health Gan Kim Yong announced a diabetes taskforce to look into preventing diabetes, screen those at risk and manage those with diabetes to prevent severe complications. Diabetes posed a huge public policy concern not just due to the medical costs incurred from managing multi-systems and organ complications from diabetes but also the substantial economic loss to people with diabetes and their families, due to loss of employment and wages. A recent qualitative study analysing the policy in the "War on Diabetes" (Ow Yong & Koe, 2021) found that there was greater public awareness of the need to combat diabetes compared to previously. However, continuing dialogues with the various clusters of policy actors remain. Moreover, there is an imperative need to foster and encourage a more positive view towards prevention and treatment of diabetes to reduce stigmatisation for those living with the condition is imperative.

Nervous System

There is a loss of neurons as an individual ages. Neurons may also shrink in size with age. Loss of neurons would lead to a decrease in brain size. However, the nervous system has a large number of neurons, more than one will ever use in a lifetime. Hence, most older adults are still able to function well despite age-related neuron loss. Nevertheless, a decline in the sensory system can be dire, for example, delay in reaction time and postural sway, may result in an increased risk of accidents and falls.

Sleep patterns would also change with age. Common complaints among older adults include frequent night awakenings, fragmented sleep, decreased deep sleep and a longer time to fall asleep. Daytime naps tend to increase with age, which can reduce the quality and efficacy of night-time sleep. As highlighted earlier, older adults can get their sleep disrupted due to urinary incontinence and frequent urination at night. Once awake, older adults find it difficult to fall asleep again. Those working with older adults need to be cognisant that sleep changes may cause older adults to exhibit anxiety and even distress over their lack of sleep or poor sleep quality. Some sleep disorders should be evaluated and treated, and not all should be attributed to age-related changes. For example, medical conditions such as obstructive sleep apnea can affect

the quality of sleep. General good sleeping habits can be emphasised to older adults to improve sleep, including:
- Reduce daytime napping.
- Exercise regularly, three to five times a week, for at least 30 minutes each time.
- Reduce water intake at least two hours and caffeine intake at least six hours before bedtime.
- Bedtime ritual such as a warm bath, aromatherapy or massage.
- If sleep does not occur within 20 minutes, get out of bed and engage in light activities such as reading or listening to music. Avoid watching television or surfing the Internet or using the mobile phone.

Musculoskeletal System

The most significant age-related changes in the musculoskeletal system would be the progressive loss of calcium from bone after the mid-30s. This would worsen for women after menopause. Women tend to lose more bone mass than men in general. If the loss of bone mass becomes great enough to result in fractures and immobility, the process is considered pathological and is the result of osteoporosis. Osteoporosis is the most common bone disease affecting older adults. Based on the Well-being of the Singapore Elderly (WiSE) study, the prevalence of seniors at risk of osteoporosis was 52 per cent in Singapore (Wang et al., 2019). This translates to approximately about 278,000 older adults in Singapore who are at risk of osteoporosis. Osteoporosis can be regarded as a silent epidemic, whereby seniors might not be aware of their condition. Individuals with low bone density are able to proceed with their life as per normal and carry out their activities of living until they sustain bone fractures, usually hip fractures. Hip fractures are associated with increased mortality and morbidity due to prolonged immobilisation and disability, thereby reducing the quality of life. Prevention is the best approach towards osteoporosis. Measures include avoiding smoking or reducing alcohol intake, regular exercising at least three times a week and eating a balanced diet with adequate calcium and vitamin D.

Ageing also affects the cartilage in the body's joints. Cartilage surfaces become rougher in joint areas receiving the greatest stress such as the kneecap. Lack of cushioning of cartilage in between joints can result in bones rubbing against each other. This would lead to considerable pain for the older adult when walking or even with movement. Reduced cartilage is due to wear and tear as one ages. Joints stiffen and skeletal muscle mass is reduced following periods of physical inactivity. In fact, muscle mass may decrease as much as one to five per cent per day of complete rest in bed. Therefore, older adults should be encouraged to engage in physical activities whenever possible.

This chapter has highlighted the physical and physiological changes that occur in the human body as one ages. As noted earlier, it is important that we recognise that there is enormous variation in the rate of ageing amongst individuals. As older adults are more susceptible to illness in later life due to physical changes, there should be greater emphasis on health promotion and disease prevention. This would empower them to feel that they have some sense of control over age-related changes. Health promotion and disease prevention will be addressed in Chapter 5.

Chapter 3

Psychological Changes with Ageing

Moses Ko

"The wiser mind mourns less for what age takes away than what it leaves behind."
William Wordsworth

Besides the physical effects of ageing, there are also psychological changes as an individual ages. Cognitive function and the neurological system deteriorate with age, even in the absence of medical problems. Common manifestations include changes in short-term memory, information processing and problem-solving skills. Learning new skills may also require a longer period of time. The changes can be affected by life and work experiences, education and cognitive engagement.

Memory
Impairments in memory occur along a spectrum, with disease processes defined as mild cognitive impairment or dementia, depending on the degree of functioning impairment in day-to-

day activities. Mild cognitive impairment may include forgetting names of acquaintances or people, as well as occasional word-finding difficulties. Remote memory such as one's own birthday, names of past prime ministers and employment history tends to remain relatively stable. Mild cognitive impairment should not have significant effects on normal function in occupational, daily and social activities. On the other hand, dementia results in impairments in day to day functioning. Dementia will be addressed in Chapter 4.

Attention

Attention is the process by which one directs mental energies to focus on tasks at hand. It is a prerequisite for higher cognitive skills. Although ageing does not reduce attention span, it was found that older adults generally perform less well on tasks that require them to filter out excessive information, multitasking or shifting attention rapidly from one topic to another. The implication for persons working with older adults is that one needs to proceed at a pace which corresponds with their attention span. For example, a nurse teaching a patient how to administer subcutaneous insulin to manage his diabetes would need to be concise in her instructions and may need to be slightly repetitive. The older adult may not be able to sustain attention to sit through an entire one-hour session and may require the nurse to come back at different intervals to teach and check back on what has been taught.

Language

Although language ability is well-maintained throughout life, comprehension of lengthy or complex messages declines with age. Hence, instructions given need to be concise and clear. It is not uncommon that physical changes with ageing such as poorer hearing can result in apparent reduction in language skills. This may be correctable by targeting hearing loss.

Intelligence

Intelligence tests appear to show a decline after age 50. This is more so with performance tests that assess fluid intelligence which includes novel, "dual-tasks" activities and perceptual-motor tasks. Comparatively stable components include vocabulary, general cultural knowledge and comprehension (crystallised intelligence). These are generally not adversely affected by age.

While intelligence is an important part of problem-solving, the latter actually involves two phases: generating and examining various alternative solutions (divergent thinking) and choosing the most appropriate one (convergent thinking). Most intelligence tests focus on convergent thinking. On the other hand, divergent thinking is more closely associated with creativity and originality. Creativity does not appear to decline with age.

Among older adults, the ability and speed of learning new things are not homogeneous. It was found that older adults with higher educational backgrounds tend to be able to learn and execute new tasks faster. However, in general, compared to younger persons they may take longer to learn new skills.

Executive Functions and Learning New Skills

Executive functions include the ability to plan, execute and evaluate complex sequences of behaviour. Age differences favour the young particularly when speed is premium. It is the loss of speed which affects older persons in mental operations of complex tasks. As noted earlier, loss of neurons occurs as part of normal ageing. This results in older adults requiring a longer time to retrieve stored information, as the speed of processing information declines with age.

The concept of neuroplasticity can be introduced at this point. It refers to the process of establishing new neural pathways during learning and practice. It has long been assumed that this occurs most prominently in a developing brain, such as in a young child. Emerging research acknowledges that while older adults may have less neuroplasticity than younger subjects, there may be other methods to facilitate their learning experience. In broad terms, strategies include harnessing past experiences, cognitive engagement and ensuring adequate cognitive intensity and load. This may involve confronting older learners with more than one task during a practice session (Pauwels, Chalavi & Swinnen, 2018). With accelerating globalisation and technological advances, learning and in particular, learning as we age, will undoubtedly be a prerequisite to remain current and function effectively in today's society.

Impact of Physical Ageing on Psychological Health

Old age is inevitable. It is natural for individuals to recall and draw comparisons with earlier stages of their lives. The physical changes of ageing, as described in Chapter 2, could affect their psychological health. A reduction in ambulatory capacity, higher propensity for injuries, increased fatigue and reduction in sensory function may have psychological impact on seniors. For example, a hike around the reservoir that one used to undertake on a daily basis five years ago is no longer performed as quickly or as easily – the senior now needs a few days of rest and recuperation before the hike can be repeated again.

Therefore, depending on a senior's perspective, age-related changes can affect his or her personal and social adjustments. If a senior has a positive outlook and prefers to focus on the positive experiences encountered or even the opportunity to enjoy this stage of life, he/she may learn to see what he/she is still capable of doing, and accept his/her conditions, possibly even with gratitude. Conversely, it is not uncommon for one to respond in denial, refusing to accept the changes as part and parcel of ageing, thus leading to discontentment and frustration.

Beyond these, the cumulative passage of time renders one more likely to be diagnosed with chronic medical conditions. There may be an increased dependence on others for assistance and the need to curtail hobbies or interests which may be too demanding for one's ageing body. Collectively, there may be disheartening psychological effects on older adults if there is a mismatch between their expectations and their functional capacity. For example, patients with chronic organ failure such as kidney failure, may be required to go for regular dialysis sessions several times a week. This places demands on their time and energy, competing with their other priorities.

Denial, anger, resentment or sadness may ensue. These emotions, coupled with other external circumstances such as a lack of social support or finances, may predispose them to mental health challenges. For some, the loss of the ability to carry out the activities which mean so much to them could be devastating, precipitating depression and even suicide. This will be further considered in Chapter 7.

However, all is not bleak. If a senior has a hopeful outlook, a strong support network, and focuses on his/her previous contributions or what he/she can continue to bring to the table, then a sense of fulfilment and contentment could well follow.

Social and Emotional Changes with Ageing

Psychological ageing is closely associated with social and emotional changes. Social networks narrow and become more selective as a senior chooses to invest in closer ties and focus less on peripheral interactions. Common social circles involve the family, the workplace or professional spheres, and communal and religious organisations. The role that a senior plays in each social circle or setting is likely to change with age.

Emotions may become more refined and less labile or unstable as one increases in self-awareness and emotional mastery (Charles & Carstensen, 2010). Furthermore, one's personality and character, though largely stable with ageing, may in fact become accentuated. For example, one who was somewhat rigid in his or her younger days may become more rigid with age. But it should be pointed out that this does not imply all seniors are rigid. Much would depend on the baseline from which one started. Thus, despite the accentuation of that personality trait, one may still be less rigid compared to a younger person.

Within the family, children would have grown up and started their own families. Consider the empty nest syndrome, which refers to a situation where parents experience a sense of grief or emptiness as their children move out of the family home. In addition, having grandchildren can affect one's identity and responsibilities. The older adult is now the most senior within the household and extended family. They may now be regarded as the pinnacle of authority and as an adviser. Yet wisdom is required to navigate this role, particularly pertaining to the upbringing of grandchildren. The senior may have to delicately balance guiding versus interfering with parenting.

With regard to employment and the workplace, in one's younger days, retirement may have been viewed as desirable. However, the reality may be less favourable, particularly if the decision is not made voluntarily, for example, as a result of retrenchment or when an employment contract is not extended. Younger, stellar individuals may have taken over the senior's previous roles, resulting in the senior feeling displaced. With decreasing roles in their work or professional arena and without the demands and expectations of employment, the increased availability of time may be a double-edged sword. It could result in seniors feeling bored or experiencing a sense of meaninglessness, that their life has no purpose. Many seniors then turn to pursuing what they may have had to sacrifice in their younger days, when parenting and careers were prioritised. Some seniors use this opportunity to travel, learn new skills or spend time on their hobbies.

A senior's accumulated wealth and financial management will also affect his or her lifestyle in later years. Economic viability can affect one's living conditions and participation in hobbies or travel. Furthermore, medical expenses can be notoriously hefty if sufficient insurance coverage was not previously obtained to provide for rainy days.

Within the community, seniors carry a wealth of experience and wisdom. Some may find themselves in advisory positions and seek to pay it back into the community, by engaging in volunteer work or religious activities. Seniors who support their community have been found to report higher levels of positive emotions and greater purpose in life (Krause, 2006).

Unfortunately, ideals may occasionally differ from reality. While there may be many plans and hopes for later years, ageing comes with the threat of declining health. With ailing health, there may be a decrease in function, an increase in the number of medical appointments or even hospitalisations. In addition, seniors tend to be required to take more medications and be subjected to side effects. This can cumulatively affect seniors' involvement and participation in social circles, adversely impacting their psychological, social and emotional well-being.

Other Considerations of Psychological Health in Ageing

Beyond an individual's own health, some seniors may experience the loss of a spouse or friends due to death and disease. Social isolation is increasingly common if there is inadequate support.

Finally, end-of-life or palliative care, death and leaving a legacy are pertinent. When one is younger, there may be a greater curiosity and contemplation of what happens after death. Yet for seniors, particularly if they have medical conditions with an approximate prognosis and dying becomes a closer reality, they may question how much more time they are left with on earth. Sometimes, it may involve a choice between life-prolonging treatments and balancing the effects on one's quality of life. Some may have a bucket list, setting out the experiences or achievements they hope to accomplish in their lifetime before passing on. These issues will be further discussed in Chapter 7.

Awareness of the above issues reminds us that understanding and managing the process of ageing requires holistic considerations that extend beyond what may be seen or quantified. It should encompass the thoughts and emotions experienced by an ageing person as well.

This chapter has highlighted the psychological changes that occur in the human body as one ages. Older adults are often misunderstood as being senile, slow and rigid compared to their younger counterparts. Knowing the psychological changes that occur in older adults sensitises us in the way we communicate and interact with seniors. Recognising the interplay between physical health and social and emotional factors in psychological health would enable us to develop a more appropriate and comprehensive approach in understanding and assisting older adults.

Chapter 4

Medical Problems of Older Adults

Moses Ko

"The good physician treats the disease; the great physician treats the patient who has the disease."
William Osler

As adults age, they become more susceptible to disease and disability due to age-related structural changes to cells and organs. Pathological changes are secondary to diseases which can reduce an individual's function more quickly than would be expected in a healthy individual. The combination of physiological changes (discussed in Chapter 2) and pathological changes predisposes an older person to frailty and consequently increased medical problems. Both physiological and pathological decline may be mitigated by stimulation in the form of a healthy lifestyle that incorporates regular exercise, an appropriate diet and cognitive engagement. Differentiating between physiological and pathological changes may not be easy but they can be identified during consultations with medical professionals.

The Trajectories of Life

A trajectory of life is a concept used to determine a likely course of life that an individual has. These are differentiated according to pre-existing medical conditions. Incurable cancer may result in a predictable pattern of rapid loss of function and death. Conversely, with chronic organ diseases such as heart failure or kidney failure, one can have a prolonged course of reduced function before eventual death. In frailty, individuals have reduced physiological reserves and consequently baseline function to begin with. This makes them easily susceptible to even small insults such as a common cold. Possessing an understanding of these possible trajectories facilitates the setting of appropriate expectations.

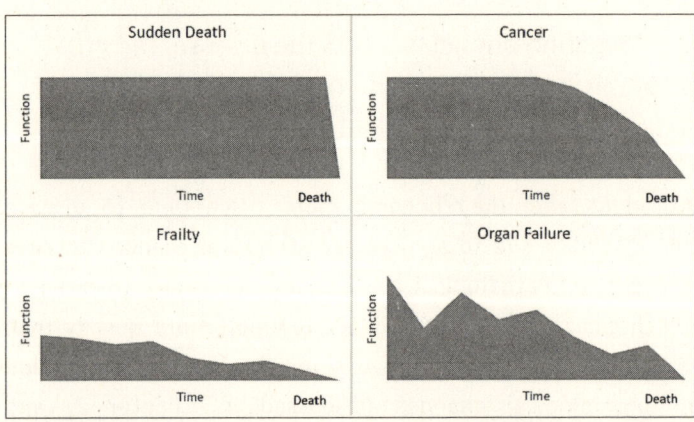

Figure 1: Trajectories of Illness

Frailty

Frailty is defined as a state of decline and increased vulnerability to adverse clinical outcomes, such as disability, delirium and falls in later life. It is associated with weakness and reduced physiological reserves. A frail older adult adapts poorly to acute illness or trauma and is vulnerable to complications. Small insults may result in disproportionately large reductions in the individual's health and functional capacity. For example, a frail community-dwelling senior who was previously able to live independently may become bedbound after a chest infection.

Frailty doubles the mortality rate among the elderly. Data from local epidemiological studies such as the Well-being of the Singapore Elderly (WiSE study) found that the prevalence of frailty amongst community-dwelling older adults was 5.7 per cent (Vaingankar et al., 2017). However, the more pressing concern was the large percentage of older adults (40.1 per cent) in the community who were at a pre-frail state. This indicates they are already on the decline and may potentially deteriorate and be at risk of adverse health outcomes (Vaingankar et al., 2017). It is important that those at risk are screened regularly with validated screening tools. Older adults who are at risk should engage in physical activity that targets strength and balance training. These would improve muscle bulk and prevent functional decline.

Geriatric Giants

The following conditions discussed below encompasses some of the "geriatric giants" or conditions that are prevalent in the elderly. This chapter will explain their background, how to recognise them, their common causes and consequences, and how these can be prevented or managed.

Falls

Background and causes

The Centre of Disease Control and Prevention reported that in 2014, 28.7 per cent of older adults reported falling (Bergen et al., 2016). Many seniors do not report a fall unless clearly asked about it. Most do not seek medical assistance unless they are seriously injured. In Singapore, falls are a leading cause of injury among older adults.

Falls may have serious consequences on older adults, particularly if they are also diagnosed with osteoporosis. This results in higher chances of fractures, the most debilitating being hip fractures. It is important to consider the predisposing factors, precipitants of the fall and complications. As noted earlier, age-related changes such as impaired vision and hearing, weaker muscle tone, slower reaction time and reduced safety awareness could increase a senior's risk of falls. Intrinsic factors such as medical conditions like frailty, stroke, Parkinson's disease, diabetes and arthritis could also increase the risk of falls. Common extrinsic or environmental factors include stairs, wires, inadequate lighting, wet floors and the use of multiple medications. Important complications to look out for when an older adult suffers a fall include injuries to the head, profuse bleeding and fractures.

Management and prevention
Management of falls would depend on the complications of the fall and identifying contributing factors. Fractures or head injuries may require older adults to undergo surgery and rehabilitation. The medical team may perform investigations to identify possible contributing factors such as infection or anaemia. The patient's medication list should be reviewed regularly to determine if unwanted side effects may be contributing to the patient's fall.

Prevention hinges on advocating a healthy lifestyle, addressing any medical conditions the patient has, avoiding unnecessary medications and minimising hazards in the older adult's environment. A healthy lifestyle includes good nutrition, keeping active and being engaged in the community. Older adults requiring home modifications can utilise the Enhancement for Active Seniors (EASE) programme, which provides subsidised home modifications such as the installation of grab bars, ramps and slip-resistant flooring. Moreover, it is important to prevent fractures as a serious complication of falls. Those with osteoporosis may be evaluated to be assessed if they could benefit from treatment.

Urinary Incontinence
Background and causes
Urinary incontinence is the loss of involuntary control of urination. Urinary incontinence may be classified as stress, urge, overflow, functional or mixed incontinence. Urinary incontinence is more common with age and in women. Common risk factors in older women include lower estrogen levels causing vaginal atrophy and multiple childbirths leading to weakened pelvic floor muscles. In men, age-related enlargement of the prostate gland can lead to both incontinence and urinary retention. Raised intra-abdominal pressure, neurological impairment and medications are also risk factors for urinary incontinence.

The psychosocial implications of urinary incontinence are perhaps the most debilitating. Sufferers may avoid leaving their homes for fear of embarrassment. This contributes to social isolation and immobility. In addition, frequent soiling of under-garments could lead to skin breakdown, rashes and wounds.

Management and prevention
Management of urinary incontinence is targeted according to the type and underlying cause of the incontinence. General measures may include reducing caffeine intake, restricting fluid intake two hours before bedtime and the use of a voiding diary to keep track of urinary elimination patterns. Pelvic floor training can increase the strength, control and coordination of pelvic muscles especially for women with stress incontinence. Medications may be prescribed for men with an enlarged prostate to manage their condition.

Postural Giddiness

Background and causes

Postural giddiness refers to giddiness experienced due to a decrease in blood pressure when one gets up, from a lying position to sitting up or from sitting to standing. The drop in blood pressure when upright is associated with decreased cerebral circulation and can result in symptoms such as dizziness, blurring of vision, weakness and even a loss of consciousness, resulting in falls. Possible causes include medications, cardiac conditions, nervous system dysfunction, endocrine conditions and volume depletion, for example, dehydration and bleeding.

Management and prevention

Management is targeted according to the underlying cause of postural hypotension. Underlying causes should be quickly identified and treated as some may be life-threatening, such as internal bleeding. Moreover, as medications are a common culprit, it is necessary to review medications and weigh their benefits and side effects. Common medications include those for hypertension, benign prostate enlargement, Parkinson's disease and pain medication. Other preventive measures include physical manoeuvres, adequate hydration, minimising rapid changes in posture and sleeping with one's head elevated. Doctors may recommend compression stockings or abdominal binders but these are not comfortable, made worse by Singapore's humid climate. Medications may be given to raise blood pressure with the aim of reducing giddiness, but these are not without their side effects.

Polypharmacy

Background and causes

Polypharmacy refers to the use of multiple medications by an individual and it is generally considered to be five or more medications daily. The risks of medication side effects and drug-drug interactions increases in such a situation. Many older adults are on multiple medications because the medications may have been started for treatment of chronic medical conditions, for general health (such as vitamins and supplements) and upon discharge from hospital. Not only do the medications interact with one another, but drug toxicity can occur more easily in the elderly due to reduced elimination and poorer compensatory function. Furthermore, the pill burden – referring to the number of medications that a patient is prescribed – can affect medication compliance.

Management and prevention
The tendency to be prescribed multiple medications is prevalent in older individuals because they may have multiple chronic illnesses. However, side effects of medications can be cumulative. This includes increasing bleeding tendencies or significantly decreasing blood pressure resulting in dizziness and falls. Medical practitioners should consider the benefit a medication provides, taking into consideration the older adult's preferences, co-morbidities, life expectancy and whether the risks involved are justified. The Beer's criteria and Screening Tool of Older Person's Prescription (STOPP) is a useful tool to assist them in making decisions regarding medications. When medications are initiated, one should "start low and go slow".

Delirium

Background and causes
Delirium is an acute-onset, fluctuating confusional state. It is common in older patients who are hospitalised. The way it manifests may vary. Though some patients may appear agitated, others may be easily overlooked as they appear to be more sleepy, quiet and withdrawn. Delirium is associated with

several adverse outcomes such as longer hospital stays, poor functional status and the need for institutionalisation, and this condition is an independent predictor for increased mortality in older patients during the 12 months after hospital admission.

Multiple factors contribute to delirium. If an individual's baseline cognitive state is impaired such as those with dementia, this significantly predisposes him or her to delirium. Some contributory factors include:

- infections;
- medications;
- falls;
- endocrine and electrolytes abnormalities;
- heart attack and stroke; and
- pain, constipation and urinary retention.

The medical team will take a detailed history, conduct a physical examination and perform appropriate investigations to decide on the likely contributing causes.

Management and prevention
Delirium has to be managed according to its underlying cause(s), while ensuring frequent environmental orientation and placing the patient in a familiar setting. For a hospitalised patient, this may involve having similar nursing staff and having familiar family members in the vicinity. The use of restraints and tethers, such as intravenous lines and urinary catheters, should be minimised when safely possible. In some tertiary hospitals such as Tan Tock Seng Hospital, there is a specialised unit known as the Geriatric Monitoring Unit (GMU) that caters to the care of patients with delirium. This ensures that optimal care can be provided for the patient with delirium.

Prevention hinges on promptly addressing contributing factors, encouraging hospitalised patients to move around regularly and the use of adaptive equipment for sensory impairments, such as spectacles and hearing aids. In addition, ensuring good hydration, nutrition, sleep, pain management and preventing constipation is necessary. Lastly, medications should be reviewed frequently.

Dementia
Background and causes
The word "dementia" originates from Latin where it broadly translates to "without (de-) the mind (mens)". Dementia is not an inevitable part of ageing. It adversely affects cognitive domains of the brain such as memory, recognition of faces and objects, speech and language, planning and executing movements, and other complex tasks such as taking care of oneself. Individuals with dementia may often forget to turn off the stove, misplace keys and these occur to an extent that their daily functioning is affected. As dementia progresses, the older adult may develop behavioural and psychological symptoms of dementia (BPSD). Behavioural symptoms include verbal and physical aggression such as cursing and hitting as well as non-aggressive behaviours such as wandering. Psychological symptoms include hallucinations, anxiety and depression.

BPSD often lead to negative outcomes for caregivers, such as high caregiver burden, stress, depression and ill health. It may also result in institutionalisation of the demented patient due to excessive caregiver stress.

Common causes of dementia include Alzheimer's dementia, vascular dementia and mixed dementia. Medical teams will evaluate the patient to exclude other conditions which may mimic dementia, as these conditions may be reversible. There is no cure for dementia but there are medications available to mitigate the decline.

Management and prevention
Though there are no measures to cure dementia, modifiable risk factors include the optimisation of cardiovascular risk factors such as control of diabetes and high blood pressure, smoking cessation, physical activity and cognitive engagement. Educating the individual and his or her loved ones is vital in helping them understand the disease and how to care for family members with dementia. Besides physical exercise and community engagement, medications can be prescribed. However, the role of medication is not for curative purposes but to slow the rate of decline of the dementia or to aid in controlling behaviour. Non-pharmacological strategies are also useful in managing symptoms of dementia such as the use of reminiscence therapy, cognitive behavioural therapy, doll therapy and music therapy. In addition, technological advances over the years have availed products to assist patients and caregivers. These may take the form of provision of reminders or tracking devices.

Depression

Background and causes
Depression is a psychiatric disorder which is characterised by a loss of interest in activities and low mood. Other features of depression may include sleep disturbances, poor appetite, fatigue, poor concentration or suicidal ideation.

In older adults, depression presents atypically, particularly with a preoccupation with minor ailments such as backache or joint pains. These conditions are common in older adults. Hence, identifying the underlying concerns patients have is paramount in building rapport, making a diagnosis and instituting appropriate treatment.

Geriatric depression has often been associated with dire consequences such as impaired daily functioning, poor quality of life and increased risk of physical illnesses due to poor management. Depression in older adults should be recognised as an important public health issue due to the risk of morbidity and suicide, as well as the high socioeconomic costs to patients, families and society, not only in Singapore but globally.

Findings from the WiSE study reported that the prevalence of depressive symptoms among older adults was 13.4 per cent (Subramaniam et al., 2016). The study findings revealed that those aged 75 or older who had lower income, poor social networks and with multiple chronic illnesses or physical disabilities have higher prevalence rates of depressive symptoms.

Management and prevention
Locally, there has been an increasing effort in prioritising the mental well-being of the elderly due to the high prevalence rates of depression and suicide amongst this group. Traditionally, treatment regimens tended to prioritise using psychiatric drugs for geriatric depression. However, in recent years, there has been wide interest in the use of counselling as a treatment modality for elderly depression. The provision of gerontological counselling is made available at Family Service Centres and various community settings. A more comprehensive discussion on the strategies and interventions to reduce the risk of geriatric depression and suicide is presented in Chapter 7.

This chapter has discussed the common diseases and medical issues experienced by older adults. It is important to be aware of the variety of health conditions that older adults are susceptible to, as they may present insidiously. Complicating this is the challenge of differentiating what is normal ageing compared to disease processes. A guiding principle would be recognising when functional changes manifest. When this happens, timely consultations with medical professionals may be required. At a minimum, it is important to cultivate healthy lifestyle habits such as having frequent exercise, a healthy and nutritious diet, and regular social and cognitive stimulation, as these could help to mitigate disease processes from developing or deteriorating.

Chapter 5

Disease Burden and Prevention

"You cannot hope to build a better world without improving the individuals. To that end each of us must work for his own improvement, and at the same time share a general responsibility for all humanity, our particular duty being to aid those to whom we think we can be most useful."

Marie Curie

In an interview with *The Straits Times* in 2015, then Deputy Prime Minister Mr Tharman Shanmugaratnam said, "Healthcare is the biggest challenge for the future of social spending. It's the fundamental reason why we need to raise more revenue, and why we have to spend effectively" (Seow, 2018). Higher healthcare spending has been attributed to the rising needs of an ageing population, due largely to the higher prevalence of chronic diseases. Chronic disease is a significant component of total claims expenditure, driving healthcare costs upward.

In Singapore, older adults are encouraged to assume personal responsibility for their own health and wellness. This includes early health screening, engaging in a healthy lifestyle and active ageing, since these play important roles in maintaining health and quality of life in the long run. In recent decades, there has been a shift in the Singapore government's focus towards more preventive healthcare measures to sustain a growing ageing population. Through the promotion of personal responsibility in the arena of health, "over-reliance on State welfare or medical insurance can be avoided" (Haseltine, 2013, p. 11).

Disease Burden
As a population ages, chronic diseases are expected to rise. It is estimated that by 2030, there will be a 33 per cent increase in diabetes prevalence, 59 per cent increase in incidences of heart attack, 70 per cent increase in people living with cancer and 110 per cent increase in stroke incidences compared to 2013 (Yuen, 2018). Chronic diseases impose an enormous financial and societal burden, and prevention is key in reducing disease burden. The Health Promotion Board (HPB) recommends several screening tests as a general guideline. These will be discussed later in this chapter.

Disease Prevention
It should be noted that normal ageing is not synonymous with illness and that illness may be preventable with modifications to health risk factors.

Disease prevention should adopt a life-course perspective using multi-sectoral and population-based approaches to reduce the prevalence of modifiable health risk factors. This includes addressing obesity, physical inactivity and unhealthy diet in the general population. It also means addressing the commercial determinants of health, such as corporations that promote products and choices that could be detrimental to health and increasing the risk of diabetes, hypertension and cardiovascular diseases.

Therefore, one of the core public policy priorities in many developed countries in recent years, including Singapore, is the promotion and maintenance of health in the elderly population (Subramaniam et al., 2019). This includes three tiers of prevention: primary, secondary and tertiary (Kisling & Das, 2021).

Primary Prevention

Primary prevention refers to preventing an individual from getting a disease. The main caveat of disease prevention is an understanding that ageing does not equate to illness and disease, and individuals can be active proponents of their own health. Primary prevention aims to educate individuals on modifiable health risk factors (MHRFs) and ways to reduce them.

MHRFs can significantly affect morbidity and mortality rates among older adults. Research has shown that MHRFs such as smoking, high-risk alcohol consumption, physical inactivity, poor nutrition and, in particular, low intake of fruits and vegetables, obesity and stress contribute significantly to mortality rates and disease incidence (Ng et al., 2020).

Older adults should be educated on good nutrition, such as having a balanced diet comprising one-quarter plate of whole grains, half a plate of fruits and vegetables and one-quarter plate of proteins (meat or alternative protein-rich food). Other nutrition tips include enhancing flavours with spices and herbs instead of salt and sugar, opting for healthier snacks such as steamed wholemeal *bao*, soft fruit (a banana or slice of papaya) or low-fat milk. Mindful, healthy eating and a balanced diet could help prevent cardiovascular disease, high blood pressure, type 2 diabetes and other chronic conditions.

Besides good nutrition, older adults need to engage in regular physical activities too. It is recommended that they engage in a combination of aerobic and strength-training exercises to maintain a healthy muscle mass. Exercise lowers the risk of chronic diseases such as heart disease, stroke and even colorectal and breast cancers. It also plays a vital role in prevention of falls and reduces the incidence of depression. Adequate exercise facilitates weight loss, increases bone density and improve cognitive functions.

Part of primary prevention also includes health vaccines. Older adults are at risk of severe disease from pneumonia if they are infected with influenza or the pneumococcal virus. Hence, it is recommended that older adults have one dose of influenza vaccine annually and one dose of pneumococcal vaccine for those aged 65 and above.

Secondary Prevention

Secondary prevention aims to reduce the impact of a disease that has already occurred. This can be done through early detection from screening and treating the disease as soon as possible to slow its progress. Screen for Life (SFL) is a national screening programme that encourages Singapore citizens to undergo regular health screening and follow up. It is free for the Pioneer generation, and costs SGD$2.00 for the Merdeka generation and those carrying the Community Health Assist Scheme (CHAS) blue or orange cards. Based on the HPB's recommendation, older adults aged 40 and above should be screened for the following conditions:

1. type 2 diabetes and cholesterol – every three years;
2. hypertension – every two years;
3. breast cancer (women) – every two years;
4. cervical cancer (women) – Pap smear every three years; and
5. colorectal cancer (both genders) – Faecal Immunochemical Test (FIT) every year.

Besides screening for chronic illnesses, there is also the availability of functional screening for older adults in the form of Project Silver Screen. It is a nationwide functional screening programme for Singaporeans aged 60 and above, which consists of three simple checks to ensure their eyes, ears and mouth are in good health.

Although existing screening programmes such as the Community Functional Screening Programme (CFSP) and SLF have been successful in raising public awareness about screening, participation rates in health screening programmes have varied take-up rates (Wong et al., 2015). In particular, cancer screening uptake has remained low among older adults. Moreover, screening programmes are least utilised by those in the lower income group (Wee et al., 2010; Wong et al., 2015). Current ways of reaching out to older adults for health screening should be evaluated to increase the take-up of these programmes.

Tertiary Prevention
Tertiary prevention aims to soften the impact of an ongoing illness that has lasting effects and improve health and quality of life for the individual living with the illness. This is carried out by helping older adults manage long-term, often-complex chronic illnesses. MOH's tertiary prevention efforts focus on ensuring that those who need care receive services in a timely manner, and seniors can continue to age in the community. MOH has increased the range of services and networks to support ageing in the community since 2016 by doubling home and community care capacity. To link up these services and provide an ecosystem of care surrounding each senior, MOH has also established the Community Networks for Seniors. This brings together various government agencies and community partners to connect health and social support for seniors. With

these initiatives, the hope is to reduce fragmented care and support seniors to live out their golden years in the community among their loved ones and friends even when they are suffering from chronic illnesses.

Health Literacy and Behaviours
In a study to assess the health screening behaviours of Singaporeans, it was reported that more than 66 per cent of the 4,337 respondents in a population-based National Health Survey have been screened at least once for chronic illnesses or cancers. However, it was found that there was lower regular screening uptake amongst lower income seniors. Factors contributing to the low uptake may not necessarily be due to screening cost (Wong et al., 2015). If cost was the only consideration, the highest health screening uptake should be amongst the lower income group as current healthcare schemes such as CHAS allows lower income seniors to undergo free health screening. The main factor influencing the decision not to screen includes fear of having to deal with greater healthcare costs if abnormal results are found and having a fatalistic attitude towards personal health. To some seniors, their attitude may be that it is best "to not know the unknown".

Fatalism is a belief that some health issues are beyond human control and encompasses beliefs such as fate, predestination and destiny. Some seniors believed that health screening for illnesses is a way of tempting fate and is a form of "bad luck". These attitudes usually stem from a lack of understanding of the etiology or cause(s) of diseases. Some seniors may also harbour the fear of being a burden to their families if they were to be diagnosed with chronic or life-threatening illnesses. These deterred them from undergoing health screening. Moreover, they may fear losing their jobs if they declare their medical illnesses. Against this backdrop, results from health screenings should be kept confidential between doctor and patient to reduce the concerns of older adults who are currently employed or plan to seek employment and do not wish to reveal the results of any illnesses to their current or potential employers. Moreover, employers could consider adopting more supportive measures and/or initiatives to enable older workers to better manage their chronic diseases and continue to contribute to their organisations.

Additionally, to address the concerns that seniors have of the costs of follow-up care and management of medical conditions, there should be partnerships with social workers in healthcare settings, silver generation ambassadors and media platforms such as SilverPages. Through outreach, they would be able to advise seniors on the available financial or funding schemes in the event that they need to undergo treatment if chronic illnesses are detected through health screening programmes.

Prevention through health screening alone does not change health literacy and human behaviours towards health. Working in partnership with other health organisations is imperative. This may include partnering with the HPB to inform older adults about healthy living and health behaviours, such as choosing food with healthy labels. This has to take place concurrently with health screenings.

To conclude, this chapter has highlighted the disease burden individuals and society face with an ageing population. It is undeniable that healthcare costs and expenditure will inevitably increase with an ageing population due to the chronic illness disease burden. Therefore, health promotion should continue to be a priority. Moreover, early detection of illnesses by means of health screening and management of chronic conditions should also be a key strategy in managing diseases. When highly subscribed to, this preventive strategy could slow down the development of late complications and disabilities in seniors. This could, in turn, prevent escalating healthcare costs. Additionally, a key strategy in reducing the high healthcare cost burden for older adults ageing in Singapore is to arrive at an optimal balance between individual responsibility, insurance coverage and government subsidies through effective healthcare policies and programmes.

Part III
Social Challenges and Integration of Seniors

Chapter 6

Social Challenges of Population Ageing I

"If you knew how unreasonably sick people suffer from reasonable causes of distress, you would take more pains about all these things."
Florence Nightingale

Societal ageing is defined as the demographic, structural and cultural transformations that a society undergoes as the ratio of older adults increases (Morgan & Kunkel, 2015). It affects every arena of society including economic growth, employment, family structure, the ability of governments and communities to provide adequate resources for older adults, and healthcare burden and costs. This chapter will focus on the changing roles of families, the stresses and strains of caregiving and end-of-life care, and offer some strategies to facilitate caregivers to cope more effectively, and inform about the available community resources.

In his 2015 Chinese New Year's message, Prime Minister Lee Hsien Loong urged Singaporeans to "build strong families as they are the bedrock of society, something generous social policies and grants alone cannot achieve" (Chan, 2015). PM Lee asserts that family ties must not weaken to the extent that the State has to supplant the family's role and take on more responsibility. In many Asian societies, the family has always been a central cultural feature. Filial piety and cultural expectations within the Asian family sets the structure for intergenerational inter-dependence (Mehta, 2007). The values that strong intergenerational ties bring to families, communities and the society as a whole are diverse and mutually beneficial. However, in a rapidly ageing modern Singapore society, the challenges confronting intergenerational relations are complex and numerous. An ageing population is altering the structures of families and the life course. Such changes also raise questions regarding the traditional contract between the generations, as well as raising queries around the reconfiguration of social institutions to deal with issues of inter- and intragenerational fairness that may arise as a consequence of population ageing. In particular, inequalities in access to health, economic and social resources – both between and within generations – are likely to remain a pressing concern over the coming decades.

Caregiving

In Singapore, families are always the first line to bear the filial responsibility of caring for their elderly. Informal caregiving, that is, care by the family or relatives, generally result in better care provision and management for the older adult and lower resource utilisation for the health and social care systems.

The Survey on Informal Caregiving (Chan et al., 2012), reported that caregivers spend long periods caring for their recipients, averaging about 38 hours per week providing physical care or ensuring care is delivered for their care recipients. Majority of caregivers in Singapore were adult children, followed by spouses and others. As in international studies, there were more female caregivers compared to male caregivers in Singapore. Women tend to stay home to provide the physical aspects of care for their parents or parents-in-law, whilst men usually provide financial support. Most female caregivers leave the workforce when their loved ones require full-time caregiving, hence they give up opportunities to further their careers. Based on the survey, there are also negative impact for those who continue working and caring for their loved ones: 29 per cent cited that they had to leave work for their care recipient's doctor's appointments and 9.6 per cent cited that they were late for work due to caregiving duties. Not uncommonly, these and other negative impact of caregiving result in stress and burnout.

Caregiver stress in Singapore may be classified into physical, emotional, social and financial stresses. Physical demands are high for care recipients who are unable to carry out day-to-day activities of living such as bathing and feeding themselves. Most of the care recipients (82 per cent) surveyed rated their health as fair or poor with an average of four chronic diseases. This implies that caregivers are required to spend long hours providing care for these seniors. Caregivers who are not trained or lack caregiving skills may also worry about not being good enough to provide the correct or proper care. Emotional stressors are high for caregivers of seniors with dementia or mental illnesses. Persons with dementia may exhibit behavioural and psychological symptoms such as aggression and hostility towards their caregivers. Those with dementia may also have wandering behaviours and caregivers need to be constantly on heightened alert for fear that their older charges may get lost or hurt.

The social impact of caregiving on caregivers includes not having enough rest and time for themselves. They may also be socially isolated if they are the only caregiver for their elderly charges. Moreover, they may be physically exhausted from caregiving duties and thus be less willing to participate in social activities. In addition, the high cost of living and continual medical expenses often put a financial strain on these adult children caring for their ageing parents. These adult children's CPF monies may also be used to fund their parents' medical bills if the older adults do not have sufficient funds in their Medisave accounts. These children in turn have to worry about their ability to fund their own retirement needs when they grow old if they have insufficient funds in their CPF accounts. Most caregivers are unable to work full-time. Hence, they are more vulnerable financially.

From the impacts listed above, there are clearly substantial personal costs and challenges to the family caregiver who is responsible for managing all the care needs of an elderly person. As a result, these caregivers often experience a significant long-term burden of care and may suffer from burnout. Caregiving often demands commitment from caregivers, such as long hours and/or responsiveness to emergencies. Caregiver burnout can lead to negative consequences such as elder abuse and caregivers themselves falling into depression. Society's expectations of caregivers to provide unpaid care for elderly parents may further reduce the country's fertility rate. Some women are concerned about facing the burden of caring for both their aged parents or parents-in-law and young children. This group is often referred to as the sandwich group. Some women may then choose to remain single or have fewer or no children to reduce the financial and physical burden of caring for both the old and young.

As the old-age support ratio of children to parents decreases, resulting in a decline in the number of children supporting a parent, filial piety should not be emphasised to the point of creating an unrealistic burden on children. Whilst the philosophy of filial responsibility which promotes care of the elderly by the family should be encouraged, there should be more support and assistance in the provision of care by the community and institutions. As stress and strains on the family increase, it is imperative for policymakers to look beyond the family and into the community. Moreover, support from the State should not be seen as a last resort but rather as a co-partner in addressing the needs of an ageing population. Involving the community goes beyond locating services and programmes for the elderly within their living vicinity. The community, such as neighbours, grassroot leaders and volunteers, could be tapped on and mobilised for available resources around an area or around networks that grow organically, and be harnessed to improve the lives of seniors. As an example, religious leaders could be tapped to identify the elderly persons' risks of depression or suicide (Ko, 2021a). Other strategies include appropriate policies at the workplace, grassroots organisations and creating physical active ageing recreational spaces to allow respite for the caregivers. Currently, more integrated housing developments for the elderly (such as Kampong Admiralty) with a wide range of social, healthcare, communal, commercial and retail facilities are being built. Given our ageing demographics and the profile of seniors, who increasingly prefer independent living rather than to co-reside with their adult children, this is a step in the right direction.

End-of-life Care
In a study entitled "Leaving Well: End-of-Life Care Policies in Singapore" conducted by the Institute of Policy Studies (IPS) in 2019, it was found that most Singaporeans want a "good death", but the majority do not get their wish (Elangovan, 2019). For example, when they think about a "good death",

an overwhelming majority imagine dying at home surrounded by loved ones, but this ideal scenario is rarely the reality. It therefore argues that much remains to be done to alter the way end-of-life care is being administered, in consideration of Singapore's rapidly ageing population, and the impact it will have on hundreds of thousands of family members needing to contend with this complex end-of-life issue.

Caring for older adults at the end of their lives could be an extremely demanding and challenging period for caregivers, as care needs intensify just before death, and this is especially so for patients with dementia (Shulz et al., 2003). Evidence suggests that caregivers who are ill-prepared for death and bereavement are less accepting of death and are at higher risk of depression, anxiety and complicated grief (Hebert et al., 2009).

Therefore, to enable caregivers to provide more effective care for their terminally ill charges, this section will first present the research findings in relation to the various domains of pain experienced by the latter, to enhance understanding about the pains of persons negotiating this final life-stage, as well as offer some tips to help caregivers facilitate a satisfactory closure to the lives of their charges. It will then discuss resources available and conclude with several approaches to assist caregivers in preparing for the deaths of their significant others and their personal bereavement subsequently.

Based on a survey of 1,200 adults 18 years or older conducted in the United States, Hinshaw (2002) observed that there were four domains of pain that reduced the quality of life for a person at the end stage of life, namely, physical, psychological or emotional, social and spiritual pain. Therefore, a uni-dimensional approach to managing symptoms does not relieve the "total pain" of such persons. This concept of total pain was first articulated by Dame Cicely Saunders, the founder of the modern hospice movement, in 1964.

Physical Pain
Physical symptoms cause distress to patients, and poor health literacy exacerbates physical pain as patient and/or caregiver do not know what questions to ask nor what to expect (Hinshaw, 2002). It was also observed that people with dementia defer decision-making to their caregivers, who frequently lack awareness of the principle of deputyship and health literacy to make informed decisions on treatment plans (Kwok et al., 2007). Deputyship will be explained later in this section.

Institutionalised patients often die in pain as there are insufficient clinicians trained to deliver palliative care (Phua et al., 2011; Finkelstein et al., 2014).

To address the above, the desired physical comfort should be provided. Care should be better coordinated, and more clinicians should be trained to offer effective palliative care to the terminally ill.

Psychological or Emotional Pain
Empirical research documented anxiety and depression as the most frequent experienced emotions amongst patients at the end-of-life stage (Kozlov et al., 2019). This may be attributed to:
- fear of impending losses in independence, autonomy, a future and all that it might bring;
- loss of self-identity;
- unfinished business; and
- coping abilities with impending death.

It was further found that those at increased psychological risk are those who are pre-occupied with the loss or having difficulty accepting the loss and/or have a history of suspected mental health issues such as depression.

The observation of impact on the mental health of patients is echoed by Jennings and colleagues, who reported that patients with dementia expressed concern about being a burden on their family near the end of their lives. Moreover, caregiver burden, particularly for dementia patients, do not always allow care arrangements to be in accordance with a patient's preference (Jennings et al., 2016). As in the preceding section, the shortage of trained clinicians in palliative care exacerbates patients' pain (Finkelstein et al., 2014; Phua et al., 2011).

Against this backdrop, the dying person should be treated with respect. Their diagnosis should be made known to them and they should be informed that they are dying, enabling them to be prepared and be provided with opportunities to fulfil their hopes, wishes and "unfinished businesses" (Lee & Tan, 2020). They should share and participate in decision-making on issues such as the preferred place of dying and death (for example, at home, in a hospice or hospital); funeral arrangements, whether to have a burial or cremation, and where it should take place; wishes such as seeing their grandchildren and significant others before death; whether to be on life support, *etc*. Some may have very specific preferences. For example, research has indicated that many Singaporean elderly have expressed a preference for dying at home (Malhotra et al., 2021).

Social Pain
Hinshaw (2002) defined social pain as the fear of separation from loved ones and broken relationships. Kozlov and colleagues further observed that dying persons who are isolated socially are at increased risk of experiencing depression and anxiety (Kozlov et al., 2019).

To address this pain, Hinshaw (2002, p. 566) noted that:

> Reconciliation is central to the work of the dying. It extends the healing they can experience beyond themselves to others. Reconciliation is the most crucial thing for the dying irrespective of whether or not the person is religious or secular. Even as their bodies are disintegrating they are becoming whole.

Indeed, the issues of reconciliation, forgiveness or unforgiveness should be addressed, particularly in relation to conflictual, ambivalent and/or problematic relationships. It is central to working with the dying (Hinshaw, 2002). Otherwise, regrets may ensue and the dying may never be able to "let go", meaning to arrive at a peaceful or satisfactory resolution and achieve a "good death". Therefore, as far as feasible, a caregiver should facilitate an opportunity for resolution, such as by informing the affected party about the impending death and arranging for a visit. If necessary, if the dying person feels he or she needs to seek forgiveness, then it might be helpful to arrange for a meeting with the offended party, in accordance with the wishes of both parties. This may bring about healing and/or some measure of closure to past hurts/misunderstandings for both.

Within the Singapore context, there appears to be some concerns by the dying person about how the family might cope when he or she passes on. This seems to be more keenly felt by older men than older women, reflecting cultural and societal norms where men have traditionally played the role of providers for their families and most older women have been homemakers. Common concerns include: "Who will my spouse (wife) live with? Is there enough to meet his/her financial needs? Is everyone doing alright? Are my children/grandchildren doing alright? Will they be able to manage?" These are usually more keenly felt by the dying senior if children are not yet married, even if they are already adults. These are pertinent issues to the dying persons and should be addressed, to allay their anxieties about the future of their loved ones, what might happen to them, how they might cope, etc, when they pass on. Where appropriate, caregivers (family or professionals) could highlight the abilities of their children and/or grandchildren that the seniors are concerned about. They could emphasise their successes and strengths, to reduce the worries of the dying person.

Therefore, social support is fundamental as care needs will increase as a person's condition deteriorates towards the end of life. As such, commitment of care as demonstrated by caregivers is crucial to the dying. This also implies that caregivers themselves would need to be supported to provide adequate care for their terminally ill relatives, having themselves to navigate through a very stressful period. More on this issue will be discussed later in this chapter.

Spiritual Pain

Hinshaw (2002, p. 565) defined spirituality as:

> ... that which allows a person to experience transcendent meaning in life. This is often expressed as a relationship with God, but it can also be about nature, art, music, family, or community – whatever beliefs and values give a person a sense of meaning and purpose in life.

In Singapore, it is not uncommon for family members to subscribe to different faiths. This could potentially lead to conflict (Lee & Tan, 2020). To address this issue, Hinshaw (2002) recommended that the spiritual history and beliefs of the terminally ill patient be considered and endorsed. This creates an avenue for him or her to discuss spiritual issues.

Another approach is to employ the Life Review method. This method was first defined by Dr Robert Butler, a world-renowned gerontologist and psychiatrist, as a "naturally occurring universal mental process, prompted by the realisation of approaching dissolution and death" (Butler, 1963, p. 66).

According to Butler, the Life Review method is useful in facilitating older persons to come to terms with unresolved issues, unfinished business and resolve them, if possible. Hinshaw (2002) added that it enables a person to identify what has been accomplished or created, as well as what will be left behind consequently, so that a sense of meaning may be captured, in recognition of the uniqueness of the individual.

Yet another method found to be effective for older adults both in the West and in Singapore is the Guided Autobiography method. Developed by Dr James Birren, Emeritus Professor of Gerontology and Psychology at the University of Southern California, it is a structured method of writing and sharing of one's life story. It enables individuals to identify, write and/or share important events and aspects of their lives by following a framework of themes such as Family, Health, Life Work, Spiritual Life and Values, Death and Dying, *etc*, by means of some guiding or priming questions for each theme. The process helps them to make meaning out of their experiences, their life stories and enables them to gain insights, as well as reinterpret past experiences. Birren's research revealed that the process is therapeutic, meaning it has healing powers. However, it is not a counselling or psychological therapy. It can be carried out individually or in a group setting with a facilitator.

The written or video/audio recorded (for those who possess low literacy levels or are unable or prefer not to write, especially older adults aged 70 or older in Singapore) autobiographies become a memento for family members and others. Other mementos that could be created by the dying persons for their family members include collections of photographs, paintings, poems, calligraphies, *etc*, which are meaningful to them. As a case example, one elderly woman in her 80s, aware that her days were numbered, decided to pen for each of her children and grandchildren Chinese idioms and proverbs which she felt were important to her, as mementos for them after her passing. In that way, she derived some psychological comfort, feeling that her values and beliefs could live on through them, thereby affirming the sense of meaning and purpose of her life.

Financial Pain

In addition to the above domains of pain, within the context of Singapore, financial pain or concerns feature prominently. A nationwide study by the Singapore Management University in 2019 (SMU, 2019), of 1,226 Singaporeans and permanent residents aged 21 years or older across age groups and ethnicities, revealed that amongst Singaporeans' fears of dying, perceived medical costs was ranked amongst the top. In relation to their life priorities at the end of life, ensuring that their illness or death will not be a financial burden to family members came up top. These findings correspond with the findings of an earlier survey carried out by the Lien Foundation in 2014. That study surveyed 1,006 Singaporeans and permanent residents aged 18 or older.

The above findings are not surprising, given the high costs of medical care in Singapore and reflects a society that subscribes to the philosophy of self-reliance and personal responsibility (or reliance on the family), and financial support at a subsistence level will only be given by the State as a last resort, unlike Western countries. Therefore, as far as possible, this issue of finance should be discussed and addressed openly, sensitively and tactfully with older adults at the end of their lives. Family members should be involved in such discussions as well.

Relevant Resources

Currently, there are various resources to support terminally ill patients and their caregivers. Some of these resources may be found in the Appendix. Other tools available are as follows:

Lasting Power of Attorney and Deputyship

Under the Mental Capacity Act, people appointed under a Lasting Power of Attorney (LPA), known as donees, are allowed to make decisions concerning life-sustaining treatment or any other treatment relating to a serious deterioration in the health of a mentally incapacitated individual.

The LPA is a legal document that provides for an individual to appoint one or more persons to act and make decisions on his/her behalf in the event that he/she has lost the mental capacity to do so himself/herself.

With more older patients deferring healthcare decisions to their family members, facilitators of advanced care planning should raise these limitations such as the loss of mental capacity when discussing end-of-life matters with individuals, and seek clarification from them on their preferences on life-sustaining treatment, and ensure that their donees, where they have executed the LPA, are informed of their preferences.

Deputyship refers to when a family court appoints an individual, known as a deputy, to make decisions on behalf of a person who lacks mental capacity where he or she has not executed an LPA. A deputy can be a family member or friend known to the person. The mental capacity of the individual has to be assessed by a medical doctor and the individual must be found to be lacking in mental capacity to make decisions due to an impairment of or disturbance in the functioning of the mind or brain.

Advance Medical Directive

An Advance Medical Directive (AMD) is a legal document that one signs to specifically inform one's doctor not to use any life-sustaining treatment to artificially prolong one's life, should death be imminent, and one is terminally ill and unconscious. Signing an AMD is entirely voluntary and can be done through a doctor. Forms for the AMD are available in polyclinics, medical clinics and hospitals. As it is a legal document, it requires two witnesses at its signing. One of the witnesses would be the doctor-in-charge and the second person has to be a suitable person aged 21 years and above. The completed form will be sent to The Registrar of the AMD.

Advance Care Plan

Unlike the AMD, an advance care plan (ACP) is not a legal document. The ACP is the process of planning for future healthcare options (Detering et al., 2010). This is done through a series of voluntary, non-legally binding conversations with an individual and his/her family and doctors. In an ACP discussion, patients are guided to understand, reflect upon and discuss their goals, values and beliefs, then led to indicate their preferences with regard to future healthcare treatments.

Strategies for Coping with Caregiving

In addition to the resources presented above, based on my research and practice, caregivers may also employ the following strategies to cope more effectively in their caregiving roles. For ease of remembering, these strategies are encapsulated in the following eight Ps:

1. Prepare

Caregivers should adopt the attitude and posture of preparation: prepare themselves, anticipate and plan ahead for the future caregiving needs of their elderly charges. These could include installation of grab bars, ramps or even preparing the impending death of the elderly (Chan & Yau, 2010). Moreover, they could also attend caregiver training programmes, to equip themselves with relevant skills, for example, effective communication, stress management and/or conflict resolution skills, end-of-life care, *etc*.

They should enhance their knowledge about the diseases of their charges, the management and treatment options, and the support services available (such as caregivers support groups), *etc*. A useful resource is the Agency for Integrated Care. For other key resources, refer to the Appendix.

2. Pause
Caregivers should learn to schedule periodic breaks to refresh and recharge themselves. They should not feel guilty about taking such breaks. Some family caregivers think that they must be available to their elderly charges at all times. Such beliefs inadvertently result in undue caregiver stress and possibly burnout.

3. Play
During these periodic breaks, caregivers should engage in activities that they enjoy and/or refreshes them. These may include spending time on their own (having "me" time) or together with their spouse or children, to play, talk, relax and laugh. Many caregivers are in the "sandwiched" generation, typically in the 30s to 50s age groups, having to juggle multiple roles and responsibilities: taking care of their young children or those still dependent on them, meeting expectations of jobs, in addition to taking care of their elderly charges. They should be mindful that their caregiving role is not the only one that they need to fulfil. Therefore, they need to learn to find an appropriate balance amongst the multiple competing demands.

4. Physical health

Maintaining good health through regular physical exercise is vital for caregivers, to sustain their caregiving roles. They should address their personal health issues to reduce their stress levels. In addition, a healthy diet with adequate nutrition is imperative to ensure they are able to offer effective care. Otherwise, if they are taken ill, who would provide care for their elderly charges?

5. Problem solving

Instead of blaming others for the health status of their older charges, adopt a problem-solving approach. For example, instead of blaming the doctors or their siblings for not doing enough for their older charges, or for not picking up signs of dementia, thus resulting in a delay in the treatment of the senior and deterioration of their condition, it would be more helpful to adopt a problem-solving mindset, set realistic goals and expectations, and be realistic about their personal capacities and competencies. These may be whether they possess the necessary skills to provide a certain type or level of nursing care if they are not trained for it, or financial resources, *etc*. If their self-assessment reveal gaps, they should seek help in meeting these gaps.

6. Praise

Caregivers could focus on what is still going on well in their lives and/or the lives of the seniors they are caring for. For example, if their siblings have been supportive, notwithstanding the fact that they may have disagreements with them about the kind of treatment their senior charges should receive, it should bring some comfort that at least these siblings do care and provide support, albeit in forms which may not be deemed ideal by the primary caregiver.

Moreover, caregivers could show appreciation and/or praise those who have assisted in the care provision, who have been supportive, who have contributed. They could also praise their elderly charges for small incremental progress. This will strengthen their motivation, for example, in physical rehabilitation.

7. Persevere
Whilst caregiving is often a stressful and long-drawn process, a "marathon" rather than a "sprint", many caregivers also reported psychological, emotional and even spiritual satisfaction from having the opportunity to provide care for their charges during this last stage of their lives. It is a "window" period for them to repay their loved ones for all they have done for them in the past, and at times to make amends and restitutions for what they have not been able to do for them in the past. Some caregivers actually relished the privilege and even acknowledged that they would not have traded it for the financial gains had they remained in their jobs.

8. Pray
Research has revealed the importance of spirituality, often expressed through prayer and finding meaning in times of hardship. Spirituality is usually accompanied by social support within the same faith group as well. Invoking spiritual beliefs and seeking solace through their faith communities often strengthen caregivers' coping capacities.

This chapter has presented several key social challenges experienced by seniors, their families and society as a consequence of population ageing. Specifically, the stresses and strains of providing day-to-day care for frail and dependent seniors, including those at the end of their lives, are considered.

Caregivers should remember that the best gift they can give to their elderly charges is to care for themselves. They would do well, therefore, to equip themselves with appropriate coping strategies, learn to accept help, mobilise and tap on existing community resources and their social support networks such as other family members and friends. This will enhance their capacity to continue to provide effective care for their elderly charges. The next chapter will discuss other key social challenges of population ageing.

Chapter 7

Social Challenges of Population Ageing II

"We've put more effort into helping folks reach old age than into helping them enjoy it."
Frank A Clark

In addition to the social challenges of population ageing presented in the preceding chapter, other key issues include elder abuse, loss, grief and bereavement, social isolation and elderly suicide. This chapter will look into these issues.

Elder Abuse
As noted earlier, families are a source of support for seniors as they age in the community. However, families can also be a source of violence, abuse and oppression. These difficulties may not be surfaced or adequately dealt with because seniors living at home are often too afraid or even embarrassed to talk about them openly to their friends and healthcare professionals. Elder abuse is a highly complex, delicate and serious human rights issue that ought to be acknowledged and addressed in society. If not dealt with adequately, it could also pose a public health

problem as elder abuse cases may result in negative health consequences for the elderly such as increased risk of morbidity and mortality, institutionalisation and hospital admissions.

Risk factors of abuse include those with cognitive impairment, poor health and functional impairment with high care needs. Abusers tend to have a history of violence, substance abuse and may have undiagnosed mental health conditions such as depression and bipolar disorder. Victims tend to be those who co-reside with their abusers and are reliant on them for financial and/or care provision. Caregiver burnout is not uncommonly a risk factor for elder abuse. Caregivers may vent their anger or frustrations on their care recipients in the heat of the moment, not realising that there can be dire consequences.

Abuse has a negative effect on families and society. However, victims are often unwilling to speak up and/or report abuse for fear of the "loss of face". In our Asian society, reporting such matters is equivalent to "airing dirty laundry in public". Even when abuse is discovered, victims may not want any intervention from the authorities, such as segregation from the abuser, as they may be dependent on the abuser for support, such as for financial and care needs. For the elderly, the fear of losing a caregiver is very real and legitimate. At times, they may be worried that by reporting the abuser, they may end up living in a nursing home, which many do not wish to do so. The desire to age-in-place, that is, continuing to live in their homes of many years, in familiar surroundings, with old friends and neighbours, is a strong sentiment among many older adults. They may also avoid disclosing the abuse for fear that the already poor or conflictual relationships with their adult children would be further jeopardised.

Studies indicate that the majority of older victims of neglect, abuse or violence are women (Yon et al., 2017). It was reported that elder abuse cases in 2018 have more than doubled in two years (Cheow & Goh, 2019). The Ministry of Social and Family Development (MSF) reported 55 cases of elder abuse in 2016 and the figures rose to 126 cases in 2018. Abusers are often family members who are caregivers of the seniors. They could be children, stepchildren or even spouses.

The various types of abuse can be classified as physical, psychological or emotional, financial and sexual abuse.

Physical

Physical abuse is the use of physical force that results in bodily injury, physical pain and even impairment in the older adult. Actions include slapping, kicking, force-feeding, restraint and use of objects to cause harm. Often physical abuse cases present in the hospital with cuts, lacerations, head injuries and bruises.

Psychological or Emotional

Psychological or emotional abuse is the infliction of anguish, emotional pain or distress. It includes constant verbal threats (such as threatening to send the older person to a nursing home) and humiliation of the elderly person. It could also include acts that cause the elderly person to have a fear of being harmed, being ignored and isolated from other family members and friends. The older adult may exhibit signs of anxiety, depression, social withdrawal and isolation.

Financial

In Singapore, cases of financial abuse may be more prevalent than reported. It is more complicated to ascertain such cases due to various common cultural practices. For example, some seniors prefer to have a joint account with their children. As many older adults are not literate or familiar with financial or legal systems, they believe that by doing so, should any mishap befall them, their children would be able to withdraw their money. The result is that, sometimes, children who are in financial difficulties may withdraw the money without the knowledge of their parents.

Another common form of financial abuse relates to property or home ownership. In Singapore, older adults sometimes sell their houses or apartments and use the proceeds to help pay for their children's apartments. They would then move in to live with their children. As the children are usually the legal owners of the new property, there have been cases whereby children abandoned their parents and refused to let them live in their homes (when relationships between them become challenging), despite their parents having previously contributed financially to the purchase of the property. Some of these children argued that since they had "accommodated" their parents for a significant period, it is their siblings' turn to take care of their parents. Such cases are usually complex and, in the eyes of the law, may or may not constitute elder abuse.

Sexual

Sexual abuse occurs when an older adult is forced to take part in an unwanted sexual activity. The perpetrators may use force, threats or take advantage of older victims who are not able to give consent, such as those who are cognitively impaired.

However, reported cases of sexual abuse in Singapore is rare. Records from the MSF revealed that there was only one case reported in 2017 and another in 2018 (Cheow & Goh, 2019). But it should be noted that such cases may be undetected or under-reported.

Recourse and Resources

When a case of elder abuse is identified, the police or a social service agency should be informed. An ambulance may need to be called if the senior's life is endangered or if he/she is injured. Following the removal of the abuser or perpetrator, the senior should be provided with community support services. The victim may be temporarily placed in alternative accommodation such as another family member's house or a nursing home. If a victim requires help with his activities of daily living such as showering, home help services may need to be arranged. The victim may also be placed in an elder daycare centre if he does not have an alternative caregiver during the day, even after moving to the home of another family member. Regardless of its duration, abuse could evoke post-traumatic stress disorder. Therefore, victims and their families should be referred for counselling. Resources such as support groups and helplines should also be provided to the victims and their families.

As elder abuse cases are very complex, a case management approach involving a multi-disciplinary team comprising a social worker/counsellor, doctor, nurse, physiotherapist, occupational therapist and law enforcers is required to manage such cases effectively. Therefore, in Singapore, a social service agency has been developed to deal with such cases. TRANS SAFE Centre is such a Family Violence Specialist Centre. It offers a range of services for people attempting to manage issues of family violence, elder abuse and elder care. It can facilitate the application for a Personal Protection Order for victims of family violence through a video link service with the Family Justice Court within the centre. Those who require assistance with such cases can contact the centre – the contact information can be found in the Appendix.

Loss, Grief and Bereavement

Loss is defined as the real or perceived deprivation of something that is meaningful to a person. Loss could occur in many forms, with loss from death being the most common. But there are also non-death losses, such as the loss of our functions due to physical or mental illnesses.

Older adults experience a variety of losses as part of life transitions. For example, the loss of a spouse or friends or loss of adult children through death or when they decide to move out of the family home, resulting in the empty nest syndrome experienced by their parents. The loss may also be due to a change of residence or retirement, resulting in a loss of income or financial security. These successive and multiple losses may have a steeling effect on them or may also demoralise them.

Grief is defined as our reaction to loss. Such reactions may be physical, psychological, emotional and/or behavioural. Bereavement refers to the objective situation of having lost someone significant. Death of a loved one is one of the most devastating life events, even more so in one's older age. It is therefore natural for older adults to experience feelings of sadness, emptiness, anger and a sense of loss after their spouse pass on. It is important to note that not all older adults experience the same trajectory when grieving. The well-known Kubler-Ross's five stages of grief, namely, denial, anger, bargaining, depression and acceptance may not be an accurate portrayal of adjustment to dying or various other losses, particularly for older adults. Some older adults may be more prepared for their own death or the death of their spouses due to long-standing illnesses. If they have lived to a relatively old age, they may see such deaths as an expected trajectory of life. Therefore, they may not experience stages such as denial or anger. It should also be noted then that grief reactions are uniquely different for individuals and often vary widely.

Nonetheless, some behaviours may be common following the loss of a loved one. Biological impact in the elderly following bereavement includes physical manifestations such as poor appetite, weight loss and non-specific pain. A significant body of research has supported the premise that negative emotions of grief reduce immune system efficiency and provokes inflammation. Stress hormones such as cortisol affects the body's cardiovascular system. Hence, it has been postulated that one may even die from a broken heart. Indeed, research has shown an increase in mortality and morbidity for those elderly individuals who have lost their spouses. In other words, the remaining widowed older adult dies soon after his or her spouse (Subramanian et al., 2008).

Psychological impact includes visual or auditory hallucinations of the dead person, guilt and feeling depressed. Studies have also revealed that the bereaved elderly who are married are more likely than the non-bereaved group to be depressed, probably because they have not only lost a spouse (primary loss) but also all the roles and tasks previously performed by the deceased spouse, such as cooking, household chores, *etc* (Subramanian et al., 2008). Behaviourally, the older person may also withdraw socially following the death of a spouse.

There are cultural differences in the way different people grieve as well. For example, some Chinese believe that one should not cry before death but may cry loudly after the departure. In the Asian and Singapore contexts, most older adults do not share their grief with their children. Thus, they may inadvertently be excluded from their family's cycle of grieving, leading to incomplete and complicated grief subsequently. However, the availability of social support such as siblings, friends and neighbours could be a buffer against the adverse impact of bereavement.

Although bereavement is a disruptive event, the majority of older adults do recover from grief. However, some seniors continue to grieve for an extended period of time and may exhibit symptoms of a state known as complicated grief. Therese Rando, a renowned clinical psychologist who has published extensively on complicated grief, noted that for parents, the loss of their children, whatever their ages, is probably the most painful. Such losses are regarded as untimely. For the elderly, the impact of such losses may even be greater, due to the compounding effects of the ageing process, deteriorations of physical and mental health, loss of functional abilities, income, *etc.*

Those assisting seniors should be aware that grief experienced by older adults is often manifested in somatic complaints (that is, complaints related to the body), particularly in the Singapore context. It is fairly common to hear older persons complaining about bodily aches and pains after various losses. This is because in our society, it is generally more acceptable to verbalise physical pains and aches than to admit one is grieving or depressed. The latter may be perceived as a sign of moral weakness or a lack of resilience. Older men, in particular, may feel the need to present a stoical front. Moreover, the current cohort of the Pioneer generation (born before 1950) and even some of the Merdeka generation (born between 1950 and 1959) generally possess lower literacy levels and limited vocabulary, compared to the younger cohorts. Therefore, many are unable to articulate their grief in psychological terms. In fact, some may not possess the psychological insights to link their various pains with their losses. Furthermore, adult children may not fully understand or appreciate the psychological pain of the older adults. In addition, by expressing their emotional pain in bodily complaints, the older adults are more likely to get the attention they want or need from their children.

In terms of counselling services for the bereaved, many of the counselling services are currently privately run and require payment. The charges are by the hour and can be substantial. The only free service currently offered is by the WiCare Support Group, which was started by a widowed lady. There are community-based counselling services such as the Samaritans of Singapore (SOS) and Sage Counselling Centre. The latter provides counselling services which are still free for seniors and their caregivers. However, such resources may not be known to older adults and their families. Therefore, more should be done to raise awareness of their availability and importance.

As issues of loss and grief are prevalent and significant in the lives of older persons, professional and family caregivers assisting older adults should be equipped with the relevant competencies to carry out grief work more effectively. These include not only helping the older person to cope with the loss, but also to manage their activities of daily living without the deceased.

Social Isolation

Generally, in Singapore, older adults hailing from the lowest income groups are not short of assistance schemes provided by the State to meet their material needs. From medical subsidies schemes and food vouchers to long-term financial assistance for public housing, many are able to get by from day to day. However, for a significant number, the greater problem lies in loneliness and social isolation as they are unable to work and are often homebound due to disabilities, failing health and/or mental illnesses. The plight of these seniors has been made worse by the COVID-19 pandemic.

Socially-isolated older adults who are poor often live in unsanitary conditions, such as homes infested with cockroaches and bedbugs. Those who live alone may not comply with their medications and may not have the health literacy to engage in preventive health measures, including consuming a healthy diet or engaging in physical exercise. They may not be known to the healthcare system or the community they live in. However, in recent years, there has been a growing community network striving to ensure that the well-being of socially-isolated seniors are taken care of and that they have social support and companionship in their final years. This network includes welfare groups, charities, hospitals' community care teams and the Senior Cluster Networks (SCN) initiated by the MSF.

SCNs are assigned by the MSF within each Housing and Development Board (HDB) town to better reach out to and support vulnerable seniors, assist them to stay engaged in the community and receive coordinated care. The SCN is operated by voluntary welfare organisations such as Fei Yue Community Services, NTUC Health, *etc*. It aims to reach out to and support vulnerable older adults, help them remain engaged in the community and receive coordinated care to facilitate ageing-in-place, that is, to age in their familiar home environment and in the community. The SCN services comprise of Senior Activity Centres (Rental and Cluster Support); Caring Assistance from Neighbours (CAN) Carers; and Senior Group Homes.

Socially-isolated seniors are misunderstood as being "stubborn". Health and social care professionals who encounter these older adults would do well to probe further about their living conditions, financial or other constraints and the issues they experience.

In addition, loss of significant others through death, migration, functional deficits and widening generation gaps may also result in older adults feeling isolated and lonely. It may be caused by alienation from one's family or environment, feeling unloved by significant others and feeling marginalised and/or disconnected to others. Loneliness, if not addressed, may result in geriatric depression and may even lead to elderly suicide.

Elderly Suicide

The World Health Organisation (WHO) estimates that each year approximately one million people die from suicide, which represents a global mortality rate of 16 people per 100,000 or one death every 40 seconds.

The major risk factors for suicide in the elderly include those who had (1) previous suicide attempts, (2) mental health conditions, (3) serious or chronic illnesses, (4) distressing life events such as death of a loved one, or (5) prolonged stress factors such as abuse or unemployment (Wong, 2018). As discussed earlier, old age is a period where one experiences successive losses. The culminating effects of chronic illnesses and worsening physical impairment could negatively affect the quality of life of a senior. Deteriorating mental health often triggers anxiety in seniors. Grief, disenfranchised grief (meaning unrecognised or unacknowledged grief) and complicated grief may result in hallucinations, depressive symptoms and may even manifest in suicidal thoughts in the elderly. Financial constraints may be more prevalent in socially-isolated seniors; they may also face rising healthcare expenses and have little savings to pay for medical fees.

The above factors may cause seniors to feel helpless and result in depressive and suicidal thoughts. Despite these struggles, many seniors avoid confiding in their family members or friends for fear of burdening them. Coupled with the common Asian belief that admitting to being depressed is a sign of "weakness", many seniors resist seeking professional help. For those who sought help, the SOS reported that elderly callers often share "their struggles with loneliness, being socially disconnected, having a fear of being a burden to their families and friends, physical and functional impairment and declining mental health" (SOS, 2018).

The SOS further reported that in 2020, the number of suicide deaths among seniors aged 60 and above hit a record high of 154, the highest recorded figure among this age group since 1991, and a 26 per cent jump from 2019. This increase could be due to the effects of the ongoing COVID-19 pandemic. Lockdown measures around the world have led to seniors being more isolated than ever. In addition, regular appointments for mental health follow-up may have been cancelled as "non-essential" services. Seniors presenting to Emergency Departments with suicidal behaviours may also be disadvantaged through overcrowding and long waiting times due to prioritisation of COVID-19 patients. This may result in sub-optimal care and follow-up, and potentially influencing elderly suicide rates.

Comparing rates across genders, more males committed suicide than females. Men tend to use more lethal methods than women when attempting suicide, thus contributing to the higher number of completed suicides amongst males (SOS, 2018). In general, the number of suicides among older men outnumber that of older women by about two to one. Men are also less likely to seek help for mental health issues as they perceive that help-seeking is associated with loss of status, identity, independence, and indicate incompetence and a loss of control and autonomy. Hence, depression may often be under-diagnosed in men and could manifest in higher depressive and suicidal symptoms.

It is concerning that whilst there was an increase in suicide deaths among seniors in 2020, SOS's 24-hour hotline received fewer calls from them. Those who called the SOS hotline expressed difficulty coping with loneliness and social isolation, psychological distress, and impaired social and family relationships resulting from the COVID-19 pandemic. The elderly who are living alone may also lack support to cope with the pandemic. Since the pandemic, many in-person activities and initiatives for the elderly, such as those at senior activity centres, have been converted to digital sessions. Those less proficient with technology may find themselves lost and unable to participate in these digital activities. Although more seniors are learning to use digital tools and platforms in recent years, many (especially those from the older cohorts) remain unaccustomed to them and prefer face-to-face interactions, to experience human touch and warmth. Therefore, digital modes of interaction continue to leave many seniors lonely and socially isolated.

For the group mentioned above, alternative means to help them connect with others would have to be explored. If they are digitally savvy, this could be achieved through various social media platforms such as Zoom, WhatsApp and video calls. These are great ways to remain connected to loved ones and friends. Most elderly persons want to hear a human voice (not a machine speaking), and they long to hear the familiar voice of a loved one. Given the uncertainty of how long the pandemic might last, it is important to build on existing efforts and to innovate and explore creative new ways to support the mental health of the elderly living in the community. This may be achieved by Silver Generation Ambassadors visiting the homes of socially-isolated individuals, whilst observing safe management measures, if applicable. Community and neighbourly efforts could be mobilised to assist in identifying potential seniors who may be at risk of social isolation and suicide. Relevant authorities should also be alerted.

This chapter and the preceding one have discussed the social issues arising from population ageing, such as caregiver burden, end-of-life care, elder abuse, grief and bereavement, social isolation and elderly suicide. If these issues are not adequately addressed, they would increase the vulnerability of seniors and their caregivers, resulting in their greater marginalisation and more pronounced social divide between the "haves" and "have nots", the "able" and "not so able" in society. Currently, we are already witnessing some signs of these (in the form of angst, frustrations, anger, *etc*), which are very costly to our society. With a rapidly ageing population, these issues are likely to worsen, unless urgent steps are taken to manage them effectively. Against this backdrop, the following two chapters will discuss various initiatives and strategies to promote the integration of seniors into our society.

Chapter 8

Strategies to Promote Social Integration I

"Age is only a number. Keep an active life."
Lailah Gifty Akita

As noted in earlier chapters, in 2016, an *Action Plan for Successful Ageing* was developed by government agencies, voluntary welfare and non-profit organisations, academia, businesses, and community and union leaders in conjunction with feedback from public consultations. The aim was for Singapore to be a "caring and inclusive society that respects and embraces seniors as an integral part of our cohesive community" (Ministry of Health [MOH], 2016a, p. 27). Three themes of successful ageing emerged:
1. opportunities for all ages;
2. kampung for all ages; and
3. city for all ages.

This chapter will look into the initiatives undertaken by the Singapore government to facilitate seniors to age-in-place, that is, within the community, in their familiar environment, to achieve their social integration.

Some of these initiatives are Integrated Home and Day Care, Senior-Friendly Housing and Schemes, and Active Ageing Hubs. These are considered in the following section.

Integrated Home and Day Care (IHDC)

In recent years, the MOH has invested substantially in growing aged care capacity and piloting new models of care.

IHDC is an integrated care model which encompasses both centre-based and home-based services, providing continuity of care for seniors at different stages of their lives. IHDC allows older adults to receive support for their illnesses and disabilities but still maintain independence by ageing in the community. Although the role of caregiving continues to fall mainly on the family, it may be eased through partnerships with different healthcare providers and community partners. The care needs of the senior is reviewed regularly by a care coordinator to ensure that care is catered for the changing needs of the seniors over time as he or she ages (Agency for Integrated Care, 2018).

The policy works on a personalised case or care management approach with a multi-disciplinary team from a service provider who will be assigned to the older adult, to decide on the type and frequency of services required (Agency for Integrated Care, 2018).

The care model for IHDC shifted the priority of medical care from a "disease-fragmented" care to "person-centric" care. The reason for a push for ageing-in-place is firstly because alternative measures such as the provision of more institutional care is unsatisfactory, both from social-emotional as well as economic perspectives (Yap, 2010). From the *National Survey of Senior Citizens 2011*, it emerged that the majority of older Singaporeans prefer to live with their children or age in the community on their own rather than in institutions (Kang et al., 2013). In a publication by the Ministry of Social and Family Development (MSF), a report on *Families and households in Singapore, 2000–2017*, it was found that the family remains as an important source of support for older adults (MSF, 2019). Amongst the older adults surveyed, 86 per cent reported they would turn to family members for physical support, 76 per cent for financial support and 79 per cent for emotional support.

Whilst the majority of adult children reported providing support for their elderly parents, there exists a small group of older adults who require State intervention, through the Commissioner for the Maintenance of Parents. This number, however, has been on a decline, from 286 cases in 2011 to 176 cases in 2017 (MSF, 2019).

Elderly family members also play an important role in physical and caregiving duties within their nuclear family unit. Based on the Survey on Social Attitudes of Singaporeans in 2016, 94 per cent of elderly respondents indicated that they provide physical support such as helping to pick up grandchildren from school or running errands for family members who need help; 97 per cent responded that they rendered emotional support by providing a listening ear or giving advice to their family members (MSF, 2019). This highlights that ageing-in-place benefits both seniors and their family members co-residing with them. Ageing-in-place enables older persons to maintain independence and autonomy, and helps them to stay connected with their immediate family members and friends. It is, therefore, reasonable to expect that future demand for home care will be greater than for institutionalised care.

Against the above backdrop, it is timely to expand such services and even offer an array of options to cater for the diverse care needs of seniors, arising from varied family and social circumstances. These services may be provided by government or publicly-funded agencies, or private providers, or a combination of both. Innovative and creative services and programmes could be pilot-tested and, if assessed to be cost-effective, be offered to provide more choices to seniors and their caregivers to further facilitate ageing-in-place. Thus, this potentially multi-million-dollar "Silver industry" could benefit private service providers too, as it is likely that an increasing number of older adults would be wealthier, as the current cohort in their 50s and 60s age. They could well afford and be prepared to pay for premium services.

Senior-Friendly Housing and Schemes
Older adults who wish to live on their own but would like to be concurrently supported with eldercare services and facilities can now opt for assisted living public housing. The newest initiative by the Government is the Community Care Apartments (CCAs), a joint offering by the Ministry of National Development (MND), the MOH and the Housing and Development Board (HDB).

CCAs are designed with senior-friendly fittings such as grab bars and a wheelchair-accessible bathroom (HDB, 2021). The CCAs project also offers communal spaces on each floor for residents to use as extensions of their own living rooms, to interact and share meals with their neighbours. Moreover, they can participate in programmes curated by the community managers in charge of the CCAs. The CCAs initiative was launched in 2021. The first batch of CCAs, located at Bukit Batok, was completed in 2021. The second batch of apartments will be located in Queenstown. It is expected to be launched in 2022. Since the majority of seniors prefer to age-in-place in the community, and considering the evidence of the benefits of such living arrangements, it is important that as a nation more of such facilities be offered to them, as far as feasible.

The HDB has also developed schemes that benefit seniors who wished to age-in-place. The Senior Priority Scheme gives priority to eligible seniors to buy 2-room Flexi flats in the same estate or near where their married children are living. Under the 2-room Flexi Scheme, seniors have the flexibility of choosing the length of lease on their 2-room Flexi flat, based on their age, needs and preferences. This can be an option for older adults to monetise their property by downsizing from their current housing unit and purchasing a new 2-room Flexi flat with a shorter-term lease. Seniors aged 55 and above can take up a lease of between 15 and 45 years in 5-year increments, as long as it covers them and their spouse up to the age of at least 95 years. Seniors can also opt for additional senior-friendly features for their flats such as built-in kitchen cabinets with induction hobs and a built-in wardrobe. The Multi-Generation Priority Scheme allows older adults to live close to their married children in the same Build-To-Order projects where 2-room Flexi or 3-room flats are integrated with other flat types.

Active Ageing Hubs
In addition to housing types and schemes, Active Ageing Hubs have been created in housing developments to encourage seniors to be physically active and socially connected as they age-in-place (MOH, 2016a). These hubs are social recreational centres that seniors living nearby in the community may drop in for activities and care services. It is a go-to place for seniors to receive timely access to basic quality healthcare, have the opportunity to build stronger social connections, take part in recreational activities such as karaoke and cooking classes, and contribute to the community through befriending and volunteering services. Active ageing is essential as it promotes physical well-being, healthy living and strengthens mental and emotional health among the elderly.

To promote social integration between the old and the young, the Singapore government has also developed intergenerational facilities within housing developments, to create a more tightly knit community across generations. Based on the *Action Plan for Successful Ageing*, there will be eldercare and childcare facilities which are co-located in ten new HDB housing developments (MOH, 2016a). The first such integrated hub was built in Kampung Admiralty in 2017, where a childcare centre, medical centre and Active Ageing Hub was located in the same building. This offered more opportunities for older adults to live, interact and play alongside the young.

This chapter has discussed the initiatives undertaken by the government of Singapore to facilitate ageing-in-place for seniors. These includes the IHDC model, housing and schemes for the elderly, and the creation of Active Ageing Hubs, targeting older adults who wish to age-in-place independently, but with the support of the community. Ageing-in-place improves the quality of life of older adults as they remain socially integrated in the communities they live in.

Chapter 9

Strategies to Promote Social Integration II

> "We are trying to construct a more inclusive society. We are going to make a country in which no one is left out."
> **Franklin D Roosevelt**

As noted in the preceding chapters, in particular Chapters 6 and 7, the ramifications and costs of population ageing to society could be high, if not addressed adequately. This chapter identifies other strategies, in addition to the initiatives undertaken by the Singapore government discussed in Chapter 8, to facilitate ageing-in-place and promote social integration of seniors and their caregivers.

Broadly, the strategies are categorised under six domains: spirituality, social support, environmental resources, early awareness and self-care, psychotherapeutic interventions and harnessing technology.

Spirituality

Studies conducted in Singapore and overseas have found spirituality to be effective in preparing and supporting the elderly through loss experiences. Research revealed that spirituality is one of the main coping mechanisms amongst Singapore elderly (Han et al., 2019) and a key determinant to successful ageing (Ng et al., 2009). Moreover, overseas studies have demonstrated that the elderly with strong spiritual beliefs experienced a quicker and more complete resolution of grief compared to those who did not hold spiritual beliefs. Research by Yale University School of Medicine revealed that those with high spirituality scores on items in the domain of intrinsic beliefs such as the importance of prayer, belief in a higher power and finding meaning in times of hardship were less likely to be depressed. Indeed, deriving comfort and strength through prayer and attendance at church, temple or mosque is an integral part of the lives of many older adults, and seniors may seek solace and support through such avenues.

In view of the important place of spirituality in the lives of older adults, religious leaders should be targeted to identify and assist those seniors at risk of depression or suicide (Ko, 2021a). Thus far, it appears that those who work in religious services or faith-based organisations have not been specifically tapped to assist such seniors. Based on my experience working with seniors, depressed seniors do seek comfort and solace from their spiritual leaders and faith communities. Therefore, this group constitutes an important resource. These leaders could be armed with basic competencies to identify warning signs and at-risk seniors. Being able to detect these and furnish seniors with information on community support services, including referral processes and contact numbers, could save their lives. Those attempting to assist seniors could mobilise these resources, thereby strengthening their abilities to navigate the various types of losses and stress experienced by them. This is even more critical in times of the current pandemic. Those who work in religious services should thus pay attention to seniors who may be in need of or crying for help.

Social Support

The importance of social support to older adults cannot be overemphasised. The level of social support received by them was observed to significantly influence their ability to cope with grieving. To elaborate, a multivariate analysis research conducted in Rio de Janeiro, Brazil (the Rio study), demonstrated that there is an association between social support and mood disorder. Non-depressed individuals were more likely to have satisfactory levels of social support. Other research also revealed a lower likelihood of depression among people with high levels of social support compared to those with low levels (Lino et al., 2013).

In Korea, depression was diagnosed in the group with low social support at three times that of those with high social support levels. In the same vein, in Thailand, the association between depression and functional incapacity was modified by the level of social support offered to them (Lino et al., 2013). Moreover, it is useful to note that it is not merely the levels of social support, but older adults' perception of the quality of social interactions that influences the likelihood of depression, as observed in a study conducted in Singapore (Lau et al., 2019).

Against this backdrop, a model to expand the social support of seniors is support groups. Research and practice evidence have demonstrated the benefits of such groups to older adults. They provide camaraderie, resources and education to those who have experienced specific losses, for example, the death of significant others, functional abilities due to various diseases, retirement, income, *etc*. Such support groups facilitate meaning-making, expression of emotions and needs. In addition, group members may feel that they are able to assist someone, as they share how they cope or navigate their loss experiences. This usually facilitates the redefinition of their roles and identities. In other words, they are not only "recipients" of help, but are also able to render help and support to others. This generally enhances their self-worth and facilitates their ability to cope with their personal losses.

However, there are several limitations associated with support groups. They are effective to the extent of the presence of good chemistry, where members feel a sense of belonging and where the group provides a safe place for sharing. Moreover, it is difficult to ensure positive interpersonal dynamics at all times, to minimise tensions and conflicts during group sessions. How effective these sessions are hinges on the skills of the facilitator of the group in managing them.

In addition to the above, within the Singapore context, where "not washing dirty linen in public", "face-saving" and "not aggravating tensions within the domestic arena" are important considerations, members might have reservations about sharing their concerns, difficulties or struggles. Selecting members who are homogenous enough, for example, with similar issues/concerns and possessing a minimum level of language (or dialect) proficiency, to facilitate mutual understanding and appreciation, or are conversant in the same dialects may not be easy too, considering the variety of languages/dialects spoken by seniors locally.

Environmental Resources

Research has found that environmental resources play a significant role in enabling independence for mobility-dependent elderly, as well as in connecting them to society, preventing further isolation and subsequent spiral into depression. For example, a recent study on the impact of environmental factors on the elderly in Singapore and Hong Kong found that (Lam et al., 2020, p. 1):

> ... in addition to one's physical health status, both objective and subjective neighbourhood factors including the size of parks, land use mix, walkability, and connectivity are all statistically significant influencing factors in geriatric depression. In particular, enhancing walkability and providing more parks at the neighbourhood level can bring mental health benefits.

It further reported that studies in Western countries found a statistically significant decrease in geriatric depression in walking-friendly neighbourhoods.

Three key variables were found to affect accessibility, namely (Lam et al., 2020):

1. Convenience: comfortable walking distance, availability of transportation, alternative routes, clear road signs, enough facilities for rest, sufficient lifts or escalators.
2. Comfort: crowded with people vs spacious for walking, sheltered walkways, no air pollution, beautification and greenery, cleanliness.
3. Safety: traffic safety, traffic light timing catering for elderly to cross the road without feeling rushed, crime condition, sidewalks conditions do not pose tripping hazard, for example, uneven or slippery surfaces, many stairs or slopes, not well lit at night.

In relation to the above, Tao and colleagues have highlighted best practices of age-friendly neighbourhoods in Singapore that possess the above attributes. Districts covered in the study were Woodlands East, Yu Hua, Waterway East, Marine Parade and Henderson Hill. In addition, the Housing and Development Board's Ease Programme (part of the Home Improvement Programme or HIP) also improves independence for the elderly, as well as persons in wheelchairs. Moreover, in general, shopping malls and MRTs are designed with ramps, lifts and escalators to enhance walkability (Tao et al., 2021).

Whilst the Singapore government should be lauded for the significant investments and progress it has achieved in improving accessibility and creating an age-friendly environment in Singapore in recent decades, these initiatives could be further strengthened to address some of the gaps, particularly in the older estates (both public and private), where many older adults are still residing in.

Early Awareness and Self-care

In a study conducted in Singapore, it was found that early awareness and preparedness were effective in reducing uncertainty, improving management of chronic conditions and thus lowering the rates of depression in late life (Mahendran et al., 2013). Early awareness brought about sustained gain in health outcomes (Lam et al., 2020). Anticipating potential stressors in advance facilitated prevention or muted the impact. Moreover, proactive coping yielded sustained gain in health outcomes.

In another study of the effect of old age on life satisfaction of Korean elderly, it was reported that preparation reduced anxiety level and generated a greater acceptance of death in the individual, as well as their family members (Kim & Kim, 2020).

The areas which are important for early awareness and preparation are as follows.

Preventive Health and Active Ageing

Physical heath was found to be closely related to an elderly person's mental well-being (Lam et al., 2020). Moreover, early awareness and/or preventive health interventions improved health-related quality of life (Ekwaru et al., 2015).

Ng and colleagues found that the salient determinants of successful ageing are: financial status, psychosocial support, spirituality and nutrition (Ng et al., 2009). These domains should be emphasised to adults well before they reach old age.

End-of-life Care and Life Review
This was discussed in Chapter 6, under the "End-of-life Care" section.

Psychotherapeutic Interventions
Beyond the above factors and approaches, to mitigate the impact of various losses which may lead to depression and/or suicide of the elderly, common and important intervention strategies include psychotherapy and counselling.

The efficacy of psychotherapy and counselling on treatment of depression and improvement on quality of life have been well documented. For example, studies have demonstrated psychotherapy/counselling intervention yielded significant improvement in depression scores (Hummel et al., 2017), and that it is just as useful as anti-depressants in the treatment of mild and moderate depression. However, a research in Singapore by Ng and colleagues found that while the efficacy of psychotherapy is generally well accepted, it is less effective in the treatment of Persistent Depressive Disorder in Singapore (Ng et al., 2016).

Some of the common approaches employed in psychotherapy and counselling are:

Expression of Losses
Invoking this approach, the focus is on facilitating individuals to be better able to identify their problems and needs, as well

as acknowledging and openly expressing them. Moreover, their concerns should be validated by others (Mehta & Ko, 2014).

Journaling is another tool employed in clinical intervention. It aids patients or clients ("clients" is a term commonly used in social and counselling services settings) by allowing them to express their emotions and needs, thus enabling a more person-centric care delivery (Caplan et al., 2005).

Meaning-making

Crisis can overwhelm the elderly, preventing those experiencing such circumstances from seeing opportunities. Therefore, facilitators and therapists play a critical role in supporting the elderly to reframe the problem and to discover direction out of the crisis they are in by challenging them to think of alternatives and in decision making.

However, the above approaches are not without their limitations. Evidence from Singapore suggests that expressions of loss encounter more barriers among the Singapore elderly compared to Western nations due to inhibiting mindsets, such as preferring not to "wash dirty linen in public". Moreover, there is still considerable stigma associated with the use of psychological counselling services, particularly among seniors (Ko, 2020a). Many older persons in their 70s and 80s hold on to traditional notions of health and healing, which include beliefs that mental health is caused by supernatural causes or problems.

Notwithstanding the above, psychotherapy and counselling, previously known as Western therapy, have made inroads into Singapore albeit adjusting to the Singapore context by "discussing religious issues or spirituality, allowing alternative therapies to complement counselling or psychotherapy, working alongside traditional healers, and inclusion of the client's family in session" (Foo et al., p. 17).

The ECADIT Model for Counselling Older Adults

The ECADIT is an evidence-based, procedural and integrative model developed in Singapore. It was developed to address a gap, as many counselling models practiced in Singapore are neither age-specific nor sensitive to accommodate the unique biological and socio-cultural conditions of older adults. Through a rigorous process of testing, role-play and role-reversal simulations, as well as refinement by local counsellors, the ECADIT model was generated.

The model is able to accommodate different theoretical orientations and is entrenched in the socio-cultural milieu of older adults in Singapore, taking into consideration the unique developmental concerns and issues of later adulthood and, significantly, it has been found to be effective for counselling older adults and their families. It is brief, simple, structured, goal-oriented and can be applied relatively easily with adequate training. It is an individualised approach that focuses on a wide range of late-life issues such as loss, grief and bereavement, depression, anxiety, interpersonal conflicts, suicidal behaviour, abuse and existential concerns. It is flexible and its pace is appropriate for older adults.

(For a full description of the ECADIT model and elder suicide intervention sub-model, refer to *Counselling Older Adults: An Asian Perspective* [Ko, 2020a].)

As noted in Chapter 7, the intersection of the vicissitudes of ageing – physical illnesses, mental health issues, multiple life-stressors and losses – compounded by the pandemic accentuating seniors' sense of loneliness and social isolation, their suicide risks are likely to increase. Within the cultural context of Singapore, where it is generally more acceptable for older adults to verbalise physical pains and illnesses than to admit some sense of depression, which may be perceived as a moral failing or a lack of resilience, there should be more targeted training of frontline healthcare professionals in primary healthcare, such as polyclinics and family clinics. Such training should cater not only to doctors, general practitioners, nurses, allied healthcare professionals such as physiotherapists, occupational therapists, it should also include TCM practitioners and pharmacists stationed at retail stores, as these typically come into frequent contact with seniors. Moreover, professionals with frequent interactions with seniors at the frontline should be equipped with appropriate communication skills, so that they are able to assess suicide risk, invoking suitable tools for such purposes.

In addition, existing suicide risk assessment tools should also be reviewed. Whilst some health and social service professionals currently utilise internationally validated, age-specific psychometric tools to assess suicide risks of seniors and for planning of follow-up care, these are often not administered due to busy clinical settings. Where feasible, these tools should be abbreviated, fine-tuned and adapted for the local context by taking into account the cultural, ethnic and religious dimensions.

Harnessing Technology
With the advent of the Fourth Industrial Revolution, rapid technological advancement, the proliferation of artificial intelligence, robotics, virtual reality and the Internet of Things, *etc*, a wide spectrum of gero-technological tools and gadgets to facilitate older adults to age-in-place have been proposed and developed (Chaudhuri et al., 2014; Pang et al, 2019; Rajagopalan et al., 2017). These technologies range from systems built into the home environment to "smart" orthotics that provide biofeedback or adaptive mechanical compensation to promote better balance or alter the centre of gravity of a patient to prevent falls. With the power and capabilities of technologies to enhance the quality of life and/or care for seniors and their

families, they should be proactively harnessed. The following section presents some examples of these tools.

Home-monitoring Systems

Home detection systems use sensors deployed in the environment to detect falls (Hemmatpour et al., 2019; Igual et al., 2013). The most common types of these systems include cameras, acoustic and pressure sensors that are usually placed in the older adult's normal environment with measurements in place to determine if the elderly has fallen in his or her home. In vision-based home fall systems, cameras are one of the key components (De Miguel et al., 2017). It is based on real-time execution of an algorithm to detect a fall based on standard computing platforms with low cost cameras in place, in the homes of seniors living alone. The images acquired from the video cameras are processed by a local workstation to automatically detect a fall. When a fall is detected, a message would be sent to emergency services. Alarm messages can also be sent to remote caregivers not residing with the user. Multiple cameras can be set up in different rooms of the user's home and connected via a network system. However, one drawback of this device is that the fall must happen within the camera's field of view, otherwise it cannot be detected.

However, the use of home-based camera systems to detect a senior's movements may be deemed as intrusive. In a study conducted in Singapore by Kong and Woods (2018) on seniors enrolled into the ShineSeniors project which consisted of a home fall detection system that employed sensors in their homes, it was found that older adults cited the idea of sensors in their home as being very foreign to them. This lack of understanding is often manifested as a fear of technology which often leads to the rejection of incorporating technology into a senior's daily life.

The advent of home fall detection-based systems has greatly improved the technology available for older adults living alone in the community. These systems ensure that when a fall is detected, it can be communicated in real-time to the relevant persons. However, the fear or resistance of embracing new technology remains a challenge for older adults. This is in part due to the lack of knowledge about how the technological systems can benefit them. This challenge could be overcome by engaging Silver Generation Ambassadors to visit the elderly who live alone at home. A survey to better understand their attitudes, fears, concerns and reasons for reluctance towards the use of technology in their homes should also be conducted. Solutions and strategies could then be developed systematically, taking into consideration the cultural, ethnic and gender dimensions as well. In addition, these ambassadors could promote the benefits of home-based fall detection systems so that older adults can continue to age-in-place.

Exoskeletons

Improving the quality of life of individuals should be a goal of modern society, currently and into the future. Quality of life studies conducted on older adults found that poor physical conditions limit daily mobility and the ability to move and work. This could negatively impact an older person physically, psychologically and even lead to social isolation. One of the main limitations in daily mobility might be the physical losses that occur due to the ageing process, which results in reduced muscle force or muscle power. These losses reduce the functional capacity and ability of older adults to perform daily tasks.

Exoskeletons are a new generation of powered technical aids to address physical and functional deficits (Grimmer et al., 2019). Exoskeletons are potential aids for physically impaired seniors of the future to prolong their ability to live independently as well as extend their working life. It is a lightweight scaffolding that fits over the user's arms, legs and torso to improve strength and speed. In Japan, exoskeletons have been prototyped to address the needs of an ageing workforce. Industries that require older adults to continue to perform manual labour could do so through the use of exoskeletons. Instead of having information sent from the brain to the legs, the exoskeletons work by sending it from the remote controller to the legs. In addition, exoskeletons can be wearable devices to prevent falls in the elderly. It is able to detect the user's gait and correct his or her gait when they detect any instability leading to a potential fall. However, exoskeletons can be troublesome to put on and older adults who are more image-conscious may not be willing to wear an exoskeleton. These are considerations for inventors to note, to increase take-up rates amongst seniors.

Telemedicine

The use of telemedicine and telehealth consultations have been a relatively new healthcare service in Singapore. Telehealth services are not limited to only video consults with doctors, there are currently physiotherapy, rehabilitation services and even audiology services provided at Ng Teng Fong General Hospital. The COVID-19 outbreak has seen an increase in the demand and usage of telemedicine over the last two years (Lai & Tang, 2020; Tan et al., 2020). This is likely due to stay home measures during the circuit breaker, social distancing measures and general public deterrence to visit hospitals for fear of being infected with the virus. Older adults were more widely affected as many had regular doctors' follow-up appointments for their chronic conditions. Telemedicine was a good alternative to protect both healthcare workers and patients from possible exposure to the highly transmissible COVID-19 virus, more so for the older population as they were at higher risk of complications and mortality from the virus (Tan et al., 2020).

However, a survey conducted by the Singapore Eye Research Institute (SERI) during the circuit breaker found that 55 per cent of 520 older adults aged 60 and above surveyed indicated that they were unlikely to use digital medical services if the COVID-19 pandemic continued (Begum, 2021). Seventy-seven per cent of the older adults surveyed said they were uncomfortable with artificial intelligence (AI) interpreting their medical tests results. These findings highlighted that older persons in Singapore may not yet be ready to embrace telehealth services. Barriers in adopting technology for health-related purposes includes a mistrust of technology, privacy concerns, design and user interface challenges (Fischer et al., 2014; Tan et al., 2020). Therefore, there needs to be continual engagement to understand and allay the fears, concerns and the scepticism which older adults may have when it comes to telehealth services.

This chapter has discussed the key factors and strategies to facilitate older adults to age-in-place and be integrated more fully into society, including the development and deployment of technological gadgets and devices to enhance the quality of their lives. The plethora of innovative tools, services, systems and processes that could potentially be developed by harnessing technology to achieve the aforementioned objectives are truly only limited by our imagination. Recognising the potentially massive Silver market, an increasing number of entrepreneurs, technopreneurs and sociopreneurs have jumped onto the band wagon and are reaping the rewards. The pace of such growth is set to increase in the future. This is a good phenomenon and should be encouraged. More incentives should be provided by the Singapore government to cultivate the development of such innovations and initiatives, to benefit more seniors, caregivers, *etc*, and achieve a win-win for all.

Part IV
Harnessing the Potential of Seniors

Chapter 10

Seniors' Employment and Financial Security

"The impact of ageism should not be underestimated. Ageism is the root of the marginalization, social exclusion and isolation of older persons. It is also intimately linked to violence and abuse against them in public and private spheres as scapegoating and stereotyping nourish subconscious motives."

Rosa Kornfeld-Matte

In tandem with the major demographic shifts resulting from the rising proportions of seniors in Singapore, older workers will become an increasingly common feature at the workplace. To sustain economic growth and in anticipation of even more changes to the world of work in the future, governments around the world have undertaken massive preparations for their country's ageing workforce. Singapore is no exception. The changes include labour market, healthcare and public pension reforms, and social security and skills development systems. Other strategies include increasing retirement ages, encouraging women's participation in the labour force and revising of immigration policies. Workplaces are adjusting to accommodate older workers. Mid-career skills upgrading, flexible and part-time work arrangements and attitudinal change among employers and management are widely promoted in Singapore, to increase labour force participation rates, as human capital is a key resource of the country.

This chapter will provide a broad overview of the ageing workforce in the Singapore context. It will then focus on the profile of Singapore's older workers, their perceptions of work and the challenges that they experience at their workplaces. The next chapter will delve deeper into the strategies that can be employed to circumvent the challenges, and harness the experience and potential of older workers. Following that, in view of the importance of lifelong learning, for the employability and employment of seniors and for any individual to function effectively on a day-to-day basis, Chapter 12 will focus on the topic of lifelong learning.

With an ageing population, there is a shrinking working-age population which raises the concern of slower economic growth (United Nations, Economic and Social Commission for Asia and the Pacific [ESCAP], 2017). A report published by the International Labour Organisation (ILO) in 2021 revealed that Asia and the Pacific's ageing labour force is a trend that is expected to become more prevalent in the region. Older labour forces will mean higher old-age dependency ratios (ILO, 2021). Singapore's median age of labour is expected to increase by more than ten years to 46.8 years, up from 33.1 years in 1990 (ILO, 2021).

Population ageing would affect Singapore's labour productivity as the proportion of the working population shrinks.

To maintain social and economic sustainability, extending working years is inevitable. Therefore, economic productivity may still be maintained by raising the retirement age. Depending on the type of work, a relatively older workforce could be more productive due to their work experiences, cumulative knowledge and expertise. However, for jobs that are more physically demanding, older workers may be less productive. But as mentioned in the earlier chapters, technological advancements can be leveraged upon to alleviate these demands on older workers.

To build an inclusive society, equal work opportunities should be accorded to older workers. Older persons who want or need to work should be enabled to remain in employment for as long as they are able to. Evidence suggests that work policies promoting the employment of older persons benefit not only older workers, but younger workers as well. Younger workers may benefit from mentorship by older workers and older workers can, in turn, learn new technology and work processes from their younger counterparts. It is therefore imperative to increase awareness of the benefits of retaining older workers in the workplace.

In Prime Minister Lee Hsien Loong's 2021 National Day Rally speech, he announced that the Singapore government will enshrine into law the current workplace anti-discrimination guidelines (Baker, 2021). The new legislation will protect employees not only on the ground of nationality or race, but also on other grounds under the purview of the Tripartite Alliance for Fair and Progressive Employment Practices (TAFEP), which includes sex, age, race, religion and disabilities. This would address many local Singaporean workers' concerns about unfair treatment compared to work pass holders (foreigners) at their companies. In particular, there appears to be growing resentment amongst Singaporean workers, as finance and IT companies are often perceived to hire more foreigners. With TAFEP's guidelines enacted as law, it is likely to result in fairer hiring practices and job opportunities for Singaporeans. This move by the Government will also signal better and fairer job opportunities for older workers in Singapore.

Profile of Older Workers

The employment rate for older residents aged 65 and above continues to rise due to efforts to raise employability amongst seniors in Singapore. Based on Singapore's 2020 labour force report, the employment rate for older residents aged 65 and above have more than doubled in the last decade, from 10.7 per cent in 1998 to 28.5 per cent in 2020 (Ministry of Manpower [MOM], 2021). This stark increase was also seen in the proportion of seniors within the labour force, with 26 per cent of the resident labour force in 2020 aged 55 or older, up from 17 per cent in 2010 (MOM, 2021, p. 24). The increase in percentage points reflects the sustained efforts in raising older workers' employability. Government and concerted tripartite efforts, including efforts by employers and the unions, have led to better employment outcomes. Today, Singapore's employment rates for older workers are more favourable compared to OECD countries (MOM, 2019). There are also increasing demand for employment in essential services like cleaning and security undertaken by seniors, amid the COVID-19 outbreak (MOM, 2021, p. 24). The top three industries with above-average proportions of older workers in their workforce, as reported in 2020, were Cleaning and Landscape (70.5 per cent), Land Transport and Supporting Services (50.4 per cent) and Food and Beverage Services (42.8 per cent).

The last decade has seen a significant rise in the percentage of women aged 60 and older in employment although, overall, fewer older women worked compared to men (MOM, 2021). This may be attributed to relatively more women being in primary care-giving roles compared to men. Women often cited family responsibilities and caregiving as the main reasons for not working.

Perceptions of Employment

A focus group discussion was carried out in 2020 by the Centre for Ageing Research and Education (CARE) to gather older persons' perceptions of work and employment (Johan & Manap, 2021). Findings from the study revealed three key motivations for older persons to continue working. These are set out below.

Achieving Health Outcomes

Participants in the focus group highlighted the physical and mental health benefits they derived from being in employment. Due to the physical demands of their job, they were able to maintain their physical health and prevent functional decline (Johan & Manap, 2021). In addition, being actively engaged in work reduced incidences of mental decline and psychological illnesses. When compared to older adults who had retired, the physical activity involved in employment was advantageous for older workers with regard to the preservation of functional health in the long run (Choi et al., 2018). Participants also viewed employment as an integral part of realising happiness in old age.

In line with the conceptual framework for Successful Ageing developed by Rowe and Kahn (1987), older people are valuable and benefit from societal engagement such as continual employment and volunteering. Social interactions and engagements through work also offer older adults meaning and purpose in life.

Continual employment may also satisfy an older person's need for "generativity", a term coined by developmental psychologist Erik Erikson in 1950. It denotes a concern for establishing and guiding the next generation. Older workers can fulfil such a desire through teaching, training and sharing skills with younger employees by working alongside them (Choi et al., 2018).

Financial Independence

Participants in the focus group also highlighted that the high cost of living in Singapore remained a motivation for them to continue in employment. Older adults in the study were cognisant about the need to prolong their savings, maintain their current standard of living and remain self-sufficient for as long as possible, so as to avoid becoming a burden in their old age, a fear harboured by them. In addition, paid work included financial benefits such as health insurance, and they would not have to tap into their own resources to finance their health expenses.

Moreover, being financially independent meant that participants did not need to rely on support from their children and other family members. Some participants feared that if they relied on support from their children, they might end up in a nursing home if their children did not have the means to care for them. The majority of seniors in the study wanted to "have a say" in their long-term care arrangements when they grow old. Financial support from children was seen as an "added bonus" and they perceived that demanding financial support from their children could cause conflict within the family. Therefore, many of them remain motivated to work, so as to continue generating an income for themselves.

Perceived Value to Employers and Organisations

Most seniors believed they were still able to significantly contribute to the labour market and society. They often highlighted qualities they possessed, that were key to organisational success. These included being loyal to an organisation, having a good work ethic, and being resilient and consistent in the work which they produced. Having worked in an organisation for a longer period of time enabled them to have institutional knowledge in assessing, diagnosing and solving problems experienced at work. Due to their expertise and exposure from varied work experiences, they possessed the skillsets required in managing staff, resolving workplace conflicts and providing mentorship for the next generation of leaders.

The above findings concurred with earlier research conducted by TAFEP, in collaboration with the United Kingdom-based Chartered Institute of Personnel and Development (TAFEP, 2013). Managers surveyed in the study reported that mature employees brought to their organisations the following benefits (TAFEP, 2013, p. 7):

1. Greater experience, higher loyalty and commitment, as well as stronger work ethics.
2. Their skills and competencies, namely better mentoring, leading and coaching skills, better knowledge of the business, transferable skills, problem-solving abilities, fewer mistakes, stronger skills base and better customer understanding.
3. Reduction in turnover and absence costs, resulting in substantial savings for the organisations.

Work-related Challenges

The COVID-19 pandemic has led to a staggering loss of jobs. Older workers are particularly vulnerable to the impact of the global pandemic on the country's economy. Job losses are expected to affect largely the middle-aged and older workers due to rapid changes at workplaces and the factors discussed below. These workers are likely to find themselves having difficulty securing new jobs and experience greater uncertainty and lower job security in industries badly affected by the pandemic. The key challenges experienced by older workers are as follows.

Ageism at Workplaces

Notwithstanding the positive employment outcomes for older workers in the last decade, there remains considerable room for improvement in terms of workplace attitudes, hiring practices and creation of more age-friendly workplaces.

The Straits Times recently reported that five employers were penalised for placing job advertisements that discriminated against age, or showed preference for a particular age group (Iau, 2020). Although the number of workplace discrimination (against age, gender and race) complaints have fallen by slightly more than half since 2016, complaints related to age discrimination are still the most common (Iau, 2020).

Extensive evidence exists which demonstrate that older employees are just as effective at work as their younger colleagues, particularly when abilities match requirements and expertise is accounted for (Beers, 2014). Moreover, fewer customer confrontations have been attributed to the presence of older workers. They tend to have better emotional control (Johnson et al., 2013), and better crisis management and problem-solving capacity (TAFEP, 2013). There is also no consistent evidence to suggest that older workers are less productive than younger workers.

Despite the evidence, there is still an overall negative bias against older workers. Research from Singapore also found that employers who held assumptions about older workers' health and abilities on the basis of their age may influence negative attitudes towards older workers (Ko, 2021b). Employers with age stereotypical views are likely to practise age-discriminatory behaviour during the hiring and job selection process. Such negative attitudes work and hiring climate demoralise and lower older workers' self-worth and dignity.

Impact of Physically Demanding Jobs

Whilst there is awareness of the positive physical and mental health benefits of employment for older workers, the impact of physically demanding jobs on them should nevertheless be acknowledged, particularly on those employed in cleaning and landscape, food and beverage, and retail industries. Research reveals that older workers who held physically demanding jobs had a higher incidence of physical health ailments, such as cardiovascular disorders, musculoskeletal disorders and other conditions arising from occupational hazards (Choi et al., 2018; Krause et al., 2015; Petersen et al., 2012). For some older workers, despite being in poor health, they need to continue working due to the lack of financial resources for old age.

Besides physical ailments, it was also reported that physical demands placed on older workers was significantly and negatively linked with mental decline, in particular, the memory and reasoning domains of cognition (Choi et al., 2018). The presence of cognitive impairment in the elderly is an important and growing individual and public health concern. In the long run, it can result in more serious consequences, such as functional impairment, increasing rates of hospitalisation and institutionalisation.

It is important to note that the health benefits of employment should not be seen as a "one-size-fits-all" situation and different job characteristics may affect workers' physical health and cognition adversely. While older workers are generally encouraged to continue in employment, if workplaces are not re-designed or re-tooled to cater for seniors, it could be detrimental to their health to remain employed in the long run. A more in-depth discussion on how the adaptation or re-designing of workplaces can be achieved will be presented in the next chapter.

Employment Conditions

Older workers who are employed by employers with negative age-stereotypical views often find themselves accepting inequitable work arrangements and conditions that do not commensurate with their work experience and capabilities (Johan & Manap, 2021). This is particularly the case when they convert from full-time to contract employment when they are rehired after the age of 62 (MOM, 2020).

By July 2022, the retirement and re-employment ages will increase to 63 and 68 years, respectively. However, Singapore's Prime Minister has urged private-sector employers to follow the public sector's lead in implementing the increased ages from 2021. The goal is that by 2030, the retirement and re-employment ages will be raised to 65 and 70, respectively. Whilst the increase in these ages should be lauded, older workers may need to settle for drastic reductions in salary and work benefits but still be expected to perform within the same job scope.

The *National Survey of Senior Citizens 2011* conducted by the Ministry of Social and Family Development reported that monthly income for male respondents aged 55 years and older was in the range of SGD$1,000–$1,999, whilst female respondents received between SGD$500–$999. Older workers' incomes were far below the national median income. In 2016, the median monthly work income of persons aged 60-plus was SGD$2,000 (compared with SGD$3,500 among the general population). Of these, about 13,500 earned less than SGD$500 a month. These workers are three times as likely as the average worker to hold low-paying jobs, for example, in the cleaning industry (Manpower Research and Statistics Department [MRSD], 2016). With contract employment, older employees may also experience insufficient health and medical insurance coverage. Against this backdrop, the Progressive Wage Model (PWM) was developed by tripartite committees (consisting of unions, employers and the Government) to uplift the wages of lower-wage workers since 2014, beginning with the cleaning sector. The PWM has been expanded to the security and landscape sectors and will be progressively rolled out to cover other sectors, such as retail, food services and waste management in the years ahead (MOM, 2022). This is a step in the right direction, to promote a more inclusive society.

Older workers often cited that they were seen as "low market value" persons and companies who re-hire them may do so out of policy obligations rather than sincerity (Johan & Manap, 2021). As a result, senior workers may feel insecure about their self-worth. They themselves may also imbibe society's negative age stereotypes about them and deem themselves as less competent or worthy than their younger counterparts. Those who hold negative age stereotype views would feel insecure about their roles in the company, and this might lead to lower motivation to work, and poorer work performances and outcomes may ensue (Rahn et al, 2021).

Digital Divide

Many seniors highlighted that technology was a challenging aspect in today's workplaces (Johan & Manap, 2021). In a survey conducted by the Infocomm Media Development Authority (IMDA), it was reported that 58 per cent of residents above 60 years old are Internet users compared to 89 per cent of all residents. Amongst all age groups, seniors were the least technologically savvy. Many senior workers felt their skills were outdated and that they were unable to keep up with technological advancements.

Despite their struggle with technology, many accepted technological change as a necessary progression, which they needed to learn and eventually embrace in order to adapt. However, seniors felt they could be better supported in their workplaces, such as having IT ambassadors who can provide patient guidance as they navigate through the technological challenges.

In the current developing environment of the Fourth Industrial Revolution, technological trends such as the Internet of Things, robotics, virtual reality and artificial intelligence are making a profound impact on workplaces. The speed of transformation and breakthroughs has no historical precedent, disrupting every industry in every country, and changing entire systems of production, as well as management in workplaces. There is thus an urgent need to close the digital gap in workplaces. It is imperative for senior workers to acquire digital skills and be comfortable with utilising digital technology.

This chapter has highlighted the demographics of Singapore's ageing workforce, older seniors' perceptions of work, as well as the challenges they experience at the workplace. As the median age in Singapore is expected to rise from 40.6 in 2010 to 53.7 in 2050 (MOM, 2021), older employees will soon become a common sight in all our workplaces. Ageist attitudes and unfair hiring practices that persist will prevent us from leveraging on their strengths and potential in the workplace. To build a fair, just and inclusive society, and considering that Singapore possesses few natural resources, it is important to recognise that human capital has become a critical resource for the economy and its future survival. This is further necessitated by the moderation of inflow of foreign workers.

Against the above backdrop, for several decades, a key strategic focus of the Government has been the maintainane of the employment and employability of its people, particularly through lifelong learning and skills development. A major goal is also to enhance the retirement adequacy of older adults. Strategies to harness an ageing workforce and lifelong learning will therefore be discussed in the next two chapters, respectively.

Chapter 11

Harnessing the Potential
of an Ageing Workforce

"The glory of the young is their strength; the grey hair of experience is the splendour of the old."
Proverbs 20: 29, *The Bible*

As discussed in the previous chapter, ageist attitudes are the main drivers of poorer employment opportunities and less than ideal work environments for seniors. Currently, many industries still fail to recognise the value of older workers. Senior workers are a talent pool that is often under-utilised because of age-related stereotypical views, assumptions and misperceptions that they are less competent, rigid and more expensive to hire.

Building an age-friendly work environment requires the concerted efforts of multiple stakeholders: individuals, corporations, employers, the Government, the unions, social service agencies, *etc*. Considering that human capital is a critical and key resource of Singapore, accentuated by the moderation of inflow of foreign labour and the reservoir of knowledge, skills and talents of seniors, a range of measures should be implemented to fully capitalise on older workers.

Drawing from my research (Ko, 2018) and additional recent findings and developments, this chapter will present a holistic framework to achieve the above. Encapsulated in five Rs, these strategies are: Re-examining attitudes, Rebalancing age structures, Redesigning workplaces, Realigning priorities and Retraining. These are elaborated below.

Re-examining Attitudes

Combating ageism is one of the four areas identified by the United Nations under their action plan for a "Decade of Healthy Ageing (2021–2030)", which aims to align global, national and local policies to improve the lives of older adults in the next decade (World Health Organisation [WHO], 2020). It is crucial to change younger workers' and employers' thoughts, attitudes and actions towards older workers. This is the first step to managing an ageing workforce successfully.

The belief that older workers are less productive is based on a common assumption that ageing leads to a decline in health and physical capacity. As highlighted earlier, research has demonstrated that age-related declines in health do not generally adversely affect older workers' performance or productivity. There is no consistent evidence either which suggests that older workers are less productive than younger workers.

To tackle ageism in workplaces, there needs to be a fundamental change in personal beliefs, assumptions and attitudes about older workers among policymakers and employers (Ko, 2021b). This implies a fundamental shift in an individual's paradigm about older workers. To achieve this, organisations can involve their employees in an exercise to examine and reflect candidly on their unconscious or subtle biases and attitudes towards older workers (Ko, 2021b). Workplaces can also create opportunities for intergenerational collaborations and promote teams comprising members of diverse age groups to work together on projects. This would enhance awareness, appreciation, respect and cooperation across the different generations. Younger counterparts could benefit from direct mentorship guidance from older employees. Workplaces that devote time to unpack biases which are not supported by research evidence and recognise the strengths of each employee regardless of age are more likely to create teams which have higher social awareness and able to achieve better teamwork across generations.

When hiring, companies should apply fair practices to all age groups, instead of privileging one group over another. Rewards and compensation should be based on merit and objective measures of performance, or functional age, and not chronological age. Remuneration for older workers should commensurate with their roles and abilities to contribute to the company, based on merit and objective criteria of performance.

Attributes or qualities of seniors should not be overlooked as well, when hiring them. These include being loyal, having higher motivation to excel and higher levels of engagement, possessing better communication skills and stronger professional networks, *etc*, compared to their younger counterparts. These qualities would likely result in a more cohesive and dynamic workforce. Research conducted by TAFEP revealed that to mitigate recruitment biases, a strategy is to utilise an interviewing panel comprising members with a diverse age composition.

Rebalancing Age Structures
To ensure the future sustainability of a business, a company should carry out a forecast of its workforce age structure. It would be expedient to select a period between five and ten years to make realistic assumptions, yet far enough into the

future so that major changes can also be illustrated. This would reveal the actual age structure of a company's workforce and its expected development in the future. It thus offers a good launchpad to determine and discuss possible human resource problems that relate to changes in the age structure.

The variables to consider in such a forecast are the size of the workforce in relation to business development, planned dismissals and organisation restructuring and recruitment. To illustrate, if older workers predominate, is the time of the probable retirement of the employees known? Is there a threat of staff bottlenecks or a loss of expertise, owing to the departure of the older workers? If middle-aged workers predominate, is it to be expected that the middle-aged workers born in the years with high birth rates will remain with the employer? To what extent are new recruits to be expected and what might the probable age distribution of the new recruits be (Morschhäuser & Sochert, 2006)? Recruitment should be based on skills and experience rather than qualifications because older employees often have expertise without qualifications (Lou et al., 2017).

Another important variable to consider is staff turnover by age group and whether the rates are likely to remain the same in the future or if changes are probable. The anticipated retirement age of older employees in the future as well as the numbers who would be retiring should be considered. Changes in statutory provisions, such as an older age of retirement, must be factored into the consideration (Morschhäuser & Sochert, 2006). This is particularly relevant in the Singapore context, where the retirement and re-employment ages will continue to increase in the coming years.

To achieve a healthy age structure, against current demographic and business imperatives, a company should examine if it proactively recruits and retains older employees. As an example, does it formulate vacancy advertisements in such a way that older persons are also targeted? Moreover, it could evaluate whether it has been successful in retaining older employees, such as by recognising and compensating them based on their contributions and performance, and by applying a fair salary structure for all employees, commensurate with their roles and performance.

Redesigning Workplaces

Studies have shown that ergonomic workplace designs are particularly important for older employees. In general, older workers have a decline in senses, physical strength and speed as they age. As highlighted in the previous chapter, physically demanding workplaces can take a toll on senior workers' health and mental well-being. Poor health among senior employees could be a result of poor-quality work practices, workplace design and poor management practices. An unsafe work environment could increase the risk of serious workplace and occupational injuries.

Workplaces should be redesigned with the use of technical, strength-increasing work aids or tools, to prevent the physical overtaxing of mature employees, thus reducing the incidence of injuries. Work culture is also important. Workplaces with continuous, non-stop production can be hazardous to not only seniors' physical and mental health and well-being, but younger workers as well. Research revealed that even micro-breaks of only one or a few minutes have an important recovery effect. It is, therefore, recommended that the more strenuous the work, the greater the need for scattered break times.

With an ageing workforce, health conditions associated with ageing will become more common in the workforce. However, this does not imply that older workers are unable to continue to contribute to the workforce. Medical advancements and the advent of technology can enable older employees with various chronic health conditions to continue to perform effectively, as research has demonstrated. They are also able to employ various "compensatory mechanisms" such as their wider and established networks, technological tools and gadgets, *etc*, to continue to perform effectively. As an example, an older educator can utilise as simple a tool as a microphone to "compensate" for his or her reduced capacity to speak loudly and for long stretches of time, compared to when he or she was younger.

Workplace health programmes should also be encouraged. With ageing, older workers are more susceptible to chronic illnesses. Health programmes enable lifestyle changes and encourage workers to stay healthy and productive even as they age. Companies should attempt to institute these as it would benefit them in the long term, since the working lifespan of older workers would be lengthened and thus experience, institutional knowledge and expertise would be retained.

Singapore's Health Promotion Board (HPB) has pioneered a novel programme by empowering bus captains to have a healthier work life. Health risk assessments are carried out at their workplaces by occupational health specialists and they are taught skills to reduce possible musculoskeletal problems. Sunglasses are provided to bus captains so that they are able to cope with glare on the road. Chronic diseases prevention and management such as healthy lifestyle practices have also been taught and disseminated in the programme. Bus depots have also started to serve healthier food in their canteens to enable healthy eating.

Realigning Priorities

With age, the priorities of older workers may change based on their health and family commitments. Older adults tend to prefer working fewer hours or shorter days. Moreover, some are required to provide physical care for their ailing aged parents or parents-in-law, or grandchildren or even children (since later marriages are increasingly common now). Therefore, flexible work arrangements would enable older workers to remain in employment, while concurrently fulfilling their other commitments. Companies could consider the needs and interests of such employees. As far as possible, they could put in place flexible work arrangements to accommodate them. Not only would such initiatives benefit older employees, but they would also enable companies to continue to tap the valuable experience, knowledge and skills of the "silver" generation, which could otherwise be lost.

The COVID-19 pandemic appears to have accelerated the pace of adoption of flexible work arrangements, which have been promoted by the Singapore government for many years. These efforts have intensified recently. Senior political leaders, tripartite partners comprising the Ministry of Manpower (MOM), the National Trades Union Congress (NTUC) and the Singapore National Employers Federation (SNEF) have called for such practices to be made permanent features (Yong, 2022).

Companies such as Singapore Post is a laudable example. It offers flexible working hours and arrangements for its employees, especially older workers who may not be able to withstand long working hours. The process of hiring and remuneration is based on merit rather than age. Such practices would engender greater motivation in workers to put in their best efforts.

Retraining

As noted earlier, the Fourth Industrial Revolution, rapid technological advancements in our society and many parts of the world imply that the pace of change in workplaces will only escalate in the future. It is, therefore, imperative and critical to constantly invest in the skilling, reskilling and upskilling of older workers, to maintain their productivity, employment and employability, as the skills they possess today will become obsolete within a short span of time.

In Singapore, older employees have been continually urged to undergo reskilling and upskilling. Local studies have revealed that many older employees would like to learn new tasks and take on new work roles, use diverse forms of learning support and are self-directed in learning. However, some may lack confidence to learn new skills and take on new forms of work despite their interest and capacities. A targeted approach is, therefore, required to offer the guidance, encouragement and support they need. In terms of training design, it was found that mature employees desire to be positioned not just as "students" but also as "resources" with valuable experiences, skills and knowledge to offer to others, even as they are learning from others (Billett et al., 2010).

While some mature employees prefer to learn through an opportunity to share information, others prefer to learn through practice, observation, listening to and working closely with other colleagues, and even on-the-job training. These employees could be positioned as both learners and facilitators who help others to learn. More details on how to effectively engage older learners and increase their participation will be presented in the next chapter on lifelong learning.

(For a more in-depth discussion of the above strategies, refer to Ko, H. [2018]. "Holistic framework for harnessing an ageing workforce in Singapore." In A. Sakamoto & J. Sung [eds.]. *Skills and the Future of Work: Strategies for Inclusive Growth in Asia and the Pacific* [pp. 100–124]. International Labour Organisation, Regional Office for Asia and the Pacific.)

To conclude, whilst it appears that some progress has been achieved in areas such as retraining and redesigning of workplaces, propelled by the array of incentives and schemes offered by the Government, and organisations being "forced" to implement flexible work arrangements as a result of the COVID-19 pandemic, much remains to be done, particularly in the area of re-examining attitudes of employers and younger employees. To achieve more significant progress in harnessing an ageing workforce, the latter is fundamental and most crucial.

Chapter 12

Lifelong Learning

> "You are never too old to set another goal or to dream a new dream."
> C. S. Lewis

Based on Singapore's *Action Plan for Successful Ageing*, lifelong learning is a key strategy to keep older adults engaged in society and promote active ageing (Ministry of Health [MOH], 2016a). This echoes the World Health Organisation's active ageing framework. Lifelong learning is considered a key approach to ensure that older adults are able to continue participating actively in society (Goh et al., 2021). Older adults who engaged in learning were found to have improved well-being, higher rated self-confidence, life satisfaction and self-efficacy (Narushima et al., 2018). Through engaging in learning, seniors can have better social integration as well as increased civic engagement. Therefore, the significance of lifelong learning cannot be over-emphasised. This chapter will discuss the various lifelong learning opportunities for seniors in Singapore, their participation rates and motivations, as well as present an award-winning evidence-based instructional model (developed in the Singapore context) for engaging seniors.

Lifelong Learning Opportunities for Seniors
National Silver Academy (NSA)

The NSA was founded in Singapore in 2016, in response to feedback from seniors that they would like to "learn for learning's sake" so as to keep their minds active and continue to remain engaged in society (MOH, 2016b).

Seniors may choose from more than 1,000 courses offered at polytechnics, universities and community-based organisations, such as Family Central and the Singapore Association for Continuing Education. A plethora of courses are offered, including Information Technology (IT), media, health and wellness, business and the arts. Seniors who are eligible can receive subsidies of up to 50 per cent of course fees for short courses conducted at post-secondary educational institutes. In addition, courses conducted by community-based organisations charge affordable course fees ranging from $50 to $150 on average, after subsidies by the Government. The NSA also promoted Intergenerational Learning Programmes (ILP) such as workshops and seminars organised by community-based organisations. ILP is led by the Council for Third Age (C3A) to facilitate intergenerational bonding through pairing of primary and/or secondary school students with seniors in a group learning environment. Through practical lessons, for example, use of technology (Skype, Facebook, *etc*), health and wellness classes such as yoga, seniors can acquire new knowledge from youths. On the other hand, youths may also learn character building, cultural traditions and history through interactions with the seniors.

SkillsFuture

SkillsFuture was initiated in 2015 as a continuous education platform for all Singaporeans (SkillsFuture Singapore, 2020). It is a national movement to provide opportunities for all Singaporeans to develop to their fullest potential at different stages of their lives, through learning and upgrading of their skills. The aim is to enhance the skills and competencies of our workforce, including seniors, to remain relevant in a highly competitive global economy.

The four key thrusts of SkillsFuture are to:
1. Help individuals make well-informed choices in education, training and careers.
2. Develop an integrated high-quality system of education and training that responds to constantly evolving needs.
3. Promote employer recognition and career development based on skills and mastery.
4. Foster a culture that supports and celebrates lifelong learning.

All Singaporeans aged 25 and above have received an opening credit of SGD$500 from January 2016. This credit will not expire. There was a further top-up of SGD$500 for those aged 25+, and SGD$1,000 for those aged 40–60, as at 31 December 2020. Additional credit can be used from 1 October 2020 and will expire on 31 December 2025, to encourage people to take early action. The credits can be used on top of existing government course subsidies to pay for a wide range of approved skills-related courses. In addition, older workers aged 40 and above will receive up to 90 per cent of course fees subsidy for SkillsFuture Singapore (SSG) courses. The aim is to incentivise older Singaporeans to enrol for these courses, to enhance their current skills and increase their employability.

Given the benefits of lifelong learning and the positive environment for older workers to engage in lifelong learning, the second part of this chapter will elaborate on the findings from a local study conducted by the Duke-NUS Centre for Ageing Research and Education (CARE). The Transitions in Health, Employment, Social Engagement and Inter-Generational Transfers in Singapore Study (THE SIGNS Study) conducted by CARE from 2016–2017 was a nationally representative longitudinal study assessing the patterns, correlates and outcomes of productive and active ageing among older Singaporeans aged 60 and above (Goh et al., 2021). Data on lifelong learning was collected from 4,549 participants aged 60 and above.

Participation Rates of Seniors in Lifelong Learning
THE SIGNS Study reported a low prevalence of lifelong learning amongst the participants with only 13.2 per cent reported having attended at least one course or training in the past year. The proportion of seniors engaged in learning was highest amongst the young-old group, aged 60–69 years old, compared to the older age groups. This could be attributed to the fact that there was a higher proportion of young-old who were still in employment compared to the old-old. There could also be a lack of lifelong learning opportunities for older adults who have retired as most courses offered were job-related courses. As more non-work related courses are launched by the NSA, there may be an increase in older adults engaging in lifelong learning.

The profile of seniors participating in lifelong learning also differs significantly by marital status, educational status, housing type and health status of older persons. Widowed older adults were the least participative in lifelong learning (7 per cent) compared to those who were single, married or divorced. It was found that those with higher education were more likely (29 per cent) to engage in learning as compared to those with no formal education (8 per cent). Those living in larger and more expensive housing such as private housing (17 per cent) had a higher proportion engaged in learning. Those with better self-rated health were also more likely to engage in learning activities. When compared between genders for their motivations for learning (work vs non-work related courses), 67 per cent of male learners cited learning for work while female learners (67 per cent) were more likely to engage in non-job related learning courses.

The findings point to significant variations among older adult learners. This thus calls for higher inclusivity when planning and implementing lifelong learning in Singapore. Promotional strategies need to reach out to all older Singaporeans across age, ethnicity, and educational, socio-economic, health, *etc*, backgrounds.

Motivations and Barriers for Lifelong Learning in Seniors

THE SIGNS Study also revealed that there were two main key themes that motivated seniors to engage in learning, as set out below.

Personal Development

Participants cited the benefits of learning such as acquiring or improving their existing skills and knowledge. They believed that learning could enrich their lives and help them stay relevant. Learning also enabled them to fulfil their interests and life purposes. In addition, learning could also be a form of pleasure (new hobby) and enabled them to be socially engaged.

Participants also cited learning as a form of self-actualisation, as they were able to accomplish something they were not able to carry out when they were younger. It was also a form of personal development, for example, learning to use social media. Moreover, it helped older adults to maintain independence and autonomy, as they were equipped with new skills, and thus did not need to rely on others.

Social Engagement and Networks

Attending classes offered the participants opportunities to strengthen their existing social network of friends and family. Moreover, learning new skills was an avenue for seniors to contribute back to society, for example, as volunteers. Lastly, they valued the ability to share their new knowledge and skills with others.

To promote greater participation of seniors in lifelong learning, it is necessary to understand the barriers or obstacles experienced by them in engaging in continuous learning. Understanding these would enhance the NSA's and SkillsFuture's ability to develop more appropriate recommendations to meet the needs of older adult learners. THE SIGNS Study revealed the following barriers.

Barriers to Continual Learning

Health

As reported above, older adults with lower self-rated health were less likely to engage in learning. Older workers with poor health, chronic illnesses and physical disabilities may not have the physical and mental capacity to undergo learning new knowledge and skills.

Negative attitudes towards ageing

Older adults who perceived that ageing led to poorer memory and lower capabilities in learning new skills tended not to participate in lifelong learning.

Conflicting commitments

Older adults who did not engage in lifelong learning cited work commitments and caregiving responsibilities as barriers for them to enrol in courses. Lack of time or incompatibility in course timings with their personal commitments were also cited.

Programme-related barriers
Older adults who did not engage in lifelong learning also cited the following reasons for not enrolling in courses:
1. Lack of course relevancy and application to daily lives
   The course content offered by the NSA might not have direct application for older learners in their job or everyday life.
2. Lack of interesting courses available
   Older adults preferred hands-on courses but some courses offered by the NSA, such as communication, did not interest them.
3. Course affordability
   Despite subsidies from the NSA and SkillsFuture, some courses still required out-of-pocket payments, which might not be affordable for those in the lower income groups.

Recommendations to Encourage Continual Learning
The study made the following recommendations.

Firstly, courses should be more affordable. In this respect, the NSA has recently introduced free or affordable bite-sized courses as well as removing the limit on subsidies, which were capped at three courses per course provider per year. This could be an incentive to encourage older persons to undertake courses. Older adults are also influenced by their social network of friends. Hence, to promote learning, course providers could consider offering attractive discounts when sign-ups are done in a group or in pairs.

Secondly, with commitments and lack of time being a major barrier to continued learning, courses can be made more accessible to homes or offered at older persons' workplaces to reduce travelling time. Courses could also be offered in community spaces frequented by older persons, such as places of worship like mosques, temples, churches, *etc*.

Lastly, it is critical for course providers to consider personal factors which may create barriers to learning, such as older workers' interests. This would assist course providers in developing learning programmes which are more relevant to the needs of older persons.

Several researchers have noted the importance of training for employability of older workers (Pillay et al., 2010). Yet, in many countries including Singapore, older workers are under-represented in training, particularly the older and less educated. Indeed, little research has been carried out on the training of older workers. Moreover, studies have revealed that older learners have expressed a desire for classroom training (Lee et al., 2008) and prefer formal training when they want to take career steps to get ahead (Fuller & Unwin, 2005). Additionally, they have emphasised the key role that an instructor plays in driving their decision to enrol in particular learning programmes (Duay & Bryan, 2008).

Against the above backdrop, research was conducted to develop a model on how to engage older learners more effectively. The award-winning study (Ko, 2020b) uncovered patterns of actions, interactions and strategies used by successful instructors to motivate and sustain older learners' interest through the entire duration of a 90-hour workplace literacy programme. Findings from the research are presented below.

An Overview of the Instructional Model for Older Adults

The research revealed that instructors dealt with classes comprising a majority of older learners by *progressively empowering* them through three phases. Taking into account their learners' social circumstances and educational backgrounds, instructors moved through these three phases, represented by three E's: Empathising, Engaging and Empowering. While the phases are sequential, they also overlapped and often occurred concurrently.

Phase One – Empathising

In the first phase, instructors attempted to empathise with learners by understanding and motivating them. In addition, by cultivating bonds with and amongst learners, they created a comfortable and supportive environment for them, with minimal fears about the learning that was to take place.

Phase Two – Engaging

In the second phase of Engaging, the instructors sought to proactively engage all the learners in all the assigned activities and tasks by insisting on their participation. Moreover, they attempted to engage learners deeply, involving them mentally, physically (bodily) and emotionally. They aligned and adapted the lesson content and strategies to fit their learners' profile, employment goals and daily social life, and were mindful in ensuring that their instructions were pitched at levels which the learners were able to comprehend. Furthermore, with awareness of age-associated decline in memory capacity and information processing abilities, they conducted their lessons at a pace that was suitable for them. They assessed learners regularly through multiple methods and were always ready to render assistance. Learner interest was sustained by ascertaining that the course content was relevant to them and that they enjoyed the learning experience. These actions resulted in a learning climate which was challenging yet supportive for learners.

Phase Three – Empowering

In the third phase of Empowering, the instructors' primary focus was to equip learners for the end-of-programme assessment. They achieved this by reviewing with learners the lessons taught, aligning lesson content to what learners may be tested on, and simulating test formats. A key strategy employed in this phase was the leveraging of learners to teach (peer teaching), assist and support one another. These strategies engendered an environment which was capability-enhancing and supportive for learners.

(For a more detailed description of the model, refer to Ko, H. (13 August 2020b). "Teaching older adults: an instructional model from Singapore." *Educational Gerontology*, 46(12), 731–745.)

Principles Distilled from the Instructional Model – Seven Rs

Based on the model, seven salient principles for instructing older learners were distilled.

These principles are encapsulated in the following seven Rs:

1. Respect

Given Singapore's Asian cultural traditions and values, instructors of older learners should accord respect to them, notwithstanding their physical and/or psychological decrements, or social circumstances, such as hailing from very low socio-economic strata, possessing very low levels of education.

2. Relevance

To increase the motivation of older learners, instructors can align content and materials to the learners' real life/work situations, so that they have practical applications and are *recognised by learners* as relevant to them. This finding is consistent with the findings of prior empirical research on adult learning, as well as THE SIGNS study cited earlier.

3. Review

Studies on memory function have shown age-associated declines in short-term memory, due to difficulties in encoding and retrieving. When encoding and retrieval strategies are provided for, such as organising the material to be remembered, the recall performance of older adults improves and comes closer to that of younger adults. Therefore, instructors of older learners need to be mindful of these declines and carry out more frequent reviews with them, compared to younger learners.

4. Regulate

A well-established finding about ageing and cognition is that older persons take a longer time to process information than younger persons. Hence, instructors ought to regulate his/her instructional speed, the amount and level of complexity of the content to be delivered during each instructional episode, to ensure comprehension and facilitate goal attainment by older learners.

5. Reciprocity

Instructors ought to recognise the wealth of experience and knowledge of older learners, and be prepared and willing to learn from them. Adopting such a position would enhance the self-esteem of older learners, as they would feel that they have something worthwhile to contribute to their instructors, too. This, in turn, enhances their self-confidence to take on new learnings.

6. Resource

Whilst the limitations of older learners should be noted, instructors can also focus on their capabilities, and leverage on them as a resource. For example, older learners may be deployed as peer teachers in a training programme or at the workplace. Research conducted in the West have found that seniors were overwhelmingly positive towards teaching their peers. Additionally, studies in Singapore and Korea revealed that seniors found learning through the assistance of a senior guide to be helpful.

7. Re-examine

Finally, and most importantly, instructors ought to critically re-examine their underlying perceptions and beliefs about older learners, and discard those unsupported by research evidence. This is because if instructors themselves subscribe to a belief that seniors are incapable of acquiring new skills and, consequently, do not impart these skills to them, this would actually become a self-fulfilling prophecy. Whilst there are, generally, age-associated physical and psychological decrements, studies have found wide inter-individual variations in cognitive functions and functional abilities amongst older adults. As such, perceptions and beliefs about them should never be based on chronological age alone.

Geragogy Guidelines

In early 2021, a set of geragogy guidelines on training older learners, developed by the Council For Third Age in collaboration with the Singapore University of Social Sciences, was launched. These guidelines recommended effective training methods and trainer traits welcomed by older learners, which may be adopted by trainers and organisations in both formal and informal settings. The goal is to enhance the learning landscape by creating a positive and inclusive learning environment. (For a more detailed presentation of the guidelines, refer to https://www.c3a.org.sg/geragogy-guidelines.)

With the acceleration of digitalisation, more seniors are embracing and adopting technology for online learning. The instructional model, principles and guidelines can also be employed for online learning programmes.

To conclude, with an escalation of the pace of change occurring not only in Singapore but across the world, lifelong learning is considered by the Singapore government to be a critical survival strategy for the country. Therefore, seniors must undertake continuous learning, not only to maintain their employment and remain employable, but also to enable them to fully participate, engage, integrate and age successfully in our society. How might the Singapore government facilitate the successful ageing of seniors in the community? Several recommendations are proposed in the next chapter.

Part V

Recommendations and Conclusion

Chapter 13

Recommendations for Public Policies

> "It's the action, not the fruit of the action, that's important. You have to do the right thing. It may not be in your power, may not be in your time, that there'll be any fruit. But that doesn't mean you stop doing the right thing. You may never know what results come of your actions, but if you do nothing, there will be no results."
>
> Mahatma Gandhi

As noted in Chapter 1, the Singapore government has, since the early 1980s, begun the process of preparing for the implications of population ageing in Singapore. Over the past several decades, recognising the pervasiveness of the impact of population ageing, a more holistic approach was adopted from 2015, led by the Ministerial Committee on Ageing. Arising from the deliberations, an *Action Plan for Successful Ageing* (Ministry of Health [MOH], 2016a) was launched. This has formed the nation's blueprint to facilitate older adults to age well in our society. This plan will be refreshed in 2022.

Rapid changes, and a very dynamic and evolving global environment, will inevitably affect Singapore. Such developments necessitate a continuous process of policy formulation, implementation and review. Engagement with as wide a spectrum of stakeholders as possible is crucial, to garner a broad and representative perspective of their concerns, issues and interests. Such an approach would also engender greater engagement, ownership and increase the probabilities of successful implementation of policies and/or programmes. Therefore, such stakeholders' consultations should involve not only the public sector, but also the private sector such as companies, employers, management and the people sectors, for example, those hailing from voluntary welfare and non-government organisations, as well as civil society. Of paramount importance are the voices of older adults themselves, as well as that of their families and caregivers, since they will be most directly affected by the recommended or proposed changes. This chapter will set out the key thrusts as articulated by Singapore's policymakers to promote successful ageing, and propose several specific strategies to further plug existing gaps to achieve this goal.

Key Thrusts to Promote Successful Ageing

Recently, the Singapore Ministry of Health (MOH) articulated that the key thrusts which guide public policy formulation are encapsulated in three Cs, specifically, Contribution, Care and Connectedness.

Contribution

The Singapore government is aware that many older adults are interested and desire to contribute for as long as they are able to so in their golden years. Generativity or a desire to "give back" to society is a positive attribute that should be encouraged, even more so in one's third age (an age where individuals are still relatively healthy, their children have grown up and they are more financially secure).

In relation to this first thrust of Contribution, the goal is to empower seniors (particularly the young-old) to continue to contribute to the community, to mobilise and harness the abilities and capabilities of seniors to assist seniors, for example, as peer teachers, para-community workers, para-counsellors, para-care managers, *etc*, whether as volunteers or paid employees, as Silver Generation Ambassadors and/or digital ambassadors. Currently, many seniors are volunteering in various programmes in primary and secondary schools (as mentors, for example). Thus, it appears that some progress has been achieved in these areas. Such initiatives and programmes should continue to be promoted and expanded. For example, older adults could be exposed to such opportunities at their workplaces, even prior to their retirement. They could play a role in volunteerism by guiding, supporting and providing care for frail older adults.

A laudable example is PSA International, which actively encourages their older employees to engage in voluntary work, as part of their corporate social responsibility initiative. The company promotes volunteerism by allocating specific workdays for staff to be involved in voluntary work: a staff could spend a workday as a driver to ferry the frail elderly from nursing homes/community hospitals, *etc*, to medical appointments. Such programmes not only contribute to the beneficiary organisations and the seniors-in-need, they are also likely to facilitate better transitioning of the older workers into their retirement. Moreover, serving as volunteers is likely to enhance their own sense of self-worth, as they would feel useful contributing to the welfare of others.

However, as emphasised in Chapter 10, in the arena of the workplace, much more effort needs to be devoted to provide opportunities for older workers to continue to contribute. In particular, outdated and stereotypical views and myths about older workers which are unsubstantiated by research and evidence should be dispelled. Within this expressed goal of promoting Contribution by seniors, the Government should continue to work proactively with employers and unions to promote inclusive practices that value older workers and harness their strengths. An even more effective strategy is for the Government to "walk the talk", taking the lead in mining "silver capital" by beginning with the public sector (Ko, 2020b). It could do so by hiring more older workers and offering them opportunities to take on mentorship and coaching roles, and showcasing these workers. This is vitally necessary if Singapore's goal is to raise retirement and re-employment ages to 65 and 70, respectively, by 2030.

Care

The next key thrust which guides public policy formulation in facilitating successful ageing, as articulated by policymakers, is Care. The focus is on providing care, particularly enhancing the preventive aspects of care. Thus, this section will discuss physical and mental health promotion, healthcare, caregiving and consider the potential of fictive kinships.

Physical and mental health promotion
Aside from adding years to life, good health is fundamental in enabling seniors to remain active and continue to thrive within their communities. Older adults with good health are more likely to be active participants in their families and within the community. Poor health in older adults will drain healthcare, social and economic resources, and exert a negative impact on society. Therefore, for several decades, Singapore has promoted healthy lifestyles, such as by increasing awareness of a healthy

diet (for example, My Healthy Plate) and the importance of engaging in physical activity (for example, the National Steps Challenge). However, modifying the behaviour patterns of older adults is not easy, particularly for those who have done little exercise earlier in life. Studies suggest that programmes would be more effective if the interventions incorporate regular contact with an experienced fitness instructor (Hawley-Hague et al., 2013; Stathi et al., 2010). Therefore, it is proposed that to increase exercise participation, policies should focus on opportunities for affordable, accessible and achievable exercises with moderate intensity in both home and community settings, accompanied by professional support. Incentivising all forms of moderate activities would also encourage older adults to lead a healthy lifestyle.

Moreover, policies to improve availability and access to healthy foods are likely to exert a positive influence on the food older adults choose to consume. For example, overconsumption of sugar is a huge contributor to obesity, diabetes and tooth decay worldwide. A major action taken by some governments, aimed at reducing the consumption of sugar, is the introduction of taxation on sugary drinks. Similar to the function of taxing tobacco to reduce tobacco use, taxing sugary drinks could be a deterrent for some individuals in consuming sugar. Such an approach could be worth considering by the Singapore government as well.

Importantly, continual emphasis should be made through public education that only by adding healthy years to life as one ages can one truly enjoy his or her sunset years.

Healthcare
Within the public hospital system, there exists a bed crunch issue. MOH has recognised this as a pertinent problem in the healthcare system which has to be addressed continually. MOH

has done well in several areas to shunt the less urgent cases to community hospitals, transitional care teams and primary healthcare providers supporting patients at homes. However, bed occupancy continues to remain high. Elderly patients have been admitted to hospital for social reasons such as neglect, caregivers' burnout and inability to cope with older persons with high care needs. Despite public announcements on government websites and mainstream media to the general public that admission to hospitals should only be reserved for emergency cases and patients who are critically ill, there remains a high volume of patients who continue to abuse the hospital system. Within the context of the COVID-19 pandemic and the surge in COVID-19 cases, hospitals are stretched beyond their capacity. Moreover, patients who are admitted to the hospitals for COVID-19 are typically elderly patients aged 60 and above.

To free up bed occupancy, the Singapore government has initiated a Home Recovery Programme (HRP) as the default care arrangement, except for those who are partially vaccinated or unvaccinated, persons aged 80 and above, and young children below the age of one. Those enrolled in HRP have access to a telemedicine provider who can assess them and prescribe necessary treatments or medications through teleconsult. This policy and process has reduced the burden on the healthcare system as well as the bed occupancy rate for COVID-19 patients. This also enables frontline healthcare workers to attend to emergency non-COVID-19 cases, so that care is rendered in a timely manner.

Given the success of HRP, the Government could consider implementing a similar programme for non COVID-19 patients in the future. Elderly patients with certain diagnoses and stable health conditions need not be cared for in the hospitals and could be cared for in the comfort of their homes with the support of a telemedicine team. By leveraging the potential of technology, treatments may be extended in the comfort of a patient's home. Many older adults have expressed their fears of being in hospital. Therefore, to be treated within their home is likely to reduce seniors' anxieties and fears of being in a hospital. This is even more pertinent for older adults suffering from dementia, since being in a familiar environment at home could reduce the likelihood of their developing delirium due to unfamiliar faces and environment.

Caregiving
In Singapore, the Government espouses the "many helping hands approach": the family, the community and the State in care provision. The family provides support for the immediate needs of the elderly, the community and the State provide the infrastructural support to the family in delivering holistic care, such as in the financial, social and health domains, and ultimately institutional care. Whilst such a comprehensive approach generally facilitates seniors to age-in-place, meaning in their homes and within the community that they are familiar with, which is generally favoured by seniors themselves, the pertinent question to address is: to what extent do family members/caregivers possess the capability and capacity to provide care and support to their elderly charges? As discussed in Chapter 6, many caregivers themselves require much support to deliver adequate care to their families.

The challenges associated with the caregiving of older adults are discussed in Chapter 6. In addition to the recommendations on expanding care for older persons through mobilising the community and through caregiver support groups, the time appears to be ripe for the provision of higher levels of financial support to family caregivers. Paid family and medical parental care leave have emerged as important strategies in the modern workplace. Workplace human resource policies such as parental leave is insufficiently comprehensive in allaying the care loads of caregivers of the elderly. If reducing the number of institutionalised older adults is a public health goal, more radical steps should be undertaken to support caregivers. Currently, paid parental care leave is not mandatory in all industries except for civil servants who are entitled to two days per calendar year. In view of the number of follow-ups an older person with chronic illnesses require, two days is barely sufficient for a caregiver in paid employment. A number of countries such as Australia, France and Germany provide longer family caregiving leave, ranging from between one week to ten days. In the long run, paid caregiving leave should be seen as an incentive to retain workers and boost overall productivity and morale of employees.

Arising from the COVID-19 pandemic, there has been a change in how companies define workplaces. Work from home (WFH) and hybrid work arrangements have become the norm for many companies. If employees are able to continue working efficiently and effectively from home, there should be no reason why flexible work arrangements cannot be implemented. Promoting flexible workplace policies throughout the working life of employees such as working from home, allowing people to enter and exit the workforce with greater ease to fulfil caregiving responsibilities would not only reduce caregiver burden, but may enable companies to attract and retain talent. In 2019, Member of Parliament for Nee Soon Group Representation Constituency, Louis Lim, gave feedback that caregivers had expressed their preference for flexible work arrangements (FWAs) over parental leave, as a more sustainable way to balance work and caregiving responsibilities. Arrangements such as telecommuting or flexible working hours offer caregivers greater flexibility, for example, if they are required to take some time off from work for ad hoc parental care duties.

The Ministry of Manpower (MOM) has rolled out grants to encourage FWAs. The budget for the Work-Life Grant has increased from $30 million to $100 million in July 2019. This scheme allows a company to receive up to $105,000 over a period of two years, to assist the company in maintaining their employees' FWAs, such as flexi-time, flexi-load or flexi-place. However, the grant works on an application basis and there are many administrative requirements for companies before they are eligible for it. If such incentives are made more seamless, more companies are likely to tap into the grant and benefit from it.

Singapore prides itself as a country that works efficiently and productively. However, with ageing demographics, it is timely for us to consider offering paid caregiving (by the family) as well as normalising a culture of flexible work arrangements. Policies and initiatives to enable and empower caregivers in juggling their multiple roles, remaining in employment while providing more effective care, would not only benefit caregivers and their care recipients but the economy as well. This is particularly vital, since human capital is critical to Singapore's survival but in short supply, aggravated by the moderation of inflow of foreign labour.

Fictive kinship
As noted earlier, demographic changes have resulted in smaller nuclear family sizes and an increasing number of single elderly and empty-nester households. These have created several social challenges, such as the issues of caregiving and social isolation.

Fictive kin is defined as family-type relationships based not on blood or marriage. Instead, such relationships are usually borne from religious groups or close friendship ties. In Singapore, fictive kins may exist in the form of neighbours as well. Fictive kins have long been recognised as elements of the social network of individuals, but it is still an area not well researched as to how these informal relationships may play a significant role in maintaining or improving the health of seniors living in the community (Jordan-Marsh & Harden, 2005).

However, with shrinking family units and older adults living longer lives, it may be timely to consider if this social capital known as fictive kinship can be developed for the community to tap on, to support older adults to age-in-place. In addition, policies should be reviewed to include not just support for family caregivers but also for fictive kins. Currently, financial subsidies such as Caregiver Training Grant (CTG) and Home Caregiving Grant are eligible only for loved ones caring for their older adults. Moreover, workplaces do not offer leave entitlements/benefits for fictive kin caring for older adults. Parental care leave is only granted to children for care of their elderly parents. Furthermore, there are no housing grants available for a fictive kin who wishes to apply for a flat to co-reside with an older adult that he or she is providing care to.

As seniors who live in the community are a very diverse group, and some may not be cared for by a family member or a foreign domestic worker, it would be useful to explore if fictive kins could play an appropriate role in caring for older adults. Within the healthcare system, such roles may entail decision-making or end-of-life care. Fictive kins could potentially expand the social network of a senior, providing social, economic and emotional capital. Research has demonstrated that seniors with higher social support such as quality relationships, financial resources and a social network tend to be healthier than individuals who lack in these areas. Failure to acknowledge or support the preferences of older adults for fictive kins may alienate the seniors living in the community and result in early institutional placements, for example, in nursing homes.

For the above to work, government policies would need to adapt to include fictive kins and recognise them as legitimate carers for older adults. Hospital and healthcare providers should also be aware of fictive kins as carers for older adults and recognise them as part of the decision-making process in relation to the care of older persons. Workplaces should also acknowledge their role and grant caregiving leave to fictive kins who are caregivers. However, it is noted that there are potential challenges. For example, a small proportion of fictive kins may exploit the financial grants for caregiving. Fictive kins are also not legally bound to care for the older person, unlike biological children who are governed by the Maintenance of Parents Act, which provides a safety net for elderly parents who require financial support.

Despite the challenges, the presence of fictive kin ties would probably become commonplace as our population ages. Policies could be formulated to ensure consent from the older person is obtained and that he or she is agreeable for a fictive kin to act as his/her carer and proxy. The benefits are likely to outweigh the costs and potential risks. Further research could be carried out to explore the feasibility of such an arrangement.

Connectedness

The third key thrust guiding policy formulation in relation to successful ageing is Connectedness. The goal that was articulated was to ensure that seniors would remain connected at multiple levels: on the ground, within the community, to their families, friends, neighbours, colleagues, *etc*. These connections may be achieved through a variety of programmes, services, grants, schemes or activities such as ActiveSG, sports events and those organised at senior activity centres. The strategy is to invoke the *kampong spirit*, expand seniors' social networks and strengthen their social, emotional and psychological resilience via physical and/or digital platforms. Through the array of initiatives and schemes implemented, Singapore appears to have attained some progress in keeping seniors connected.

Intergenerational integration

However, as noted in Chapter 7, the rate of elderly suicide and the impact of social isolation on the elderly suggest that much remains to be done to strengthen these connections. As emphasised, social support and networks are critical factors in helping older adults cope more effectively with various losses and depression. In an ageing society, conflict can arise between the young and the old. With the increasing number of nuclear families, grandparents now have fewer opportunities to interact with their married children and grandchildren. Communication breakdowns and intergenerational tensions have been observed between the generations, impeded by language barriers, since many older adults speak only dialects while the younger generations are more comfortable speaking in English. These phenomena further heighten seniors' sense of isolation and alienation.

Therefore, going forward, it is timely for Singapore to consider embarking on a major intergenerational integration initiative. Appropriate educational policies could be developed and implemented to promote more intergenerational interactions and mutual understanding and support. A report published by the Stanford Center for Longevity highlighted that older adults could be key to helping young people develop their talents and knowledge, and provide advice on life conflicts and relationships (Beamish & Wolfe, 2016). With their wealth of experience, older people are repositories of knowledge and wisdom, and are therefore well-positioned to play the roles of champion and mentor to youths and children. They could complement family relationships and provide important support where family structures are weak. Moreover, they could step in to offer the emotional stability that many youths of today lack, due to decreasing parental presence in their lives, contributed in part by pressures to make a living. Many older adults are motivated to contribute to the lives and well-being of the younger and future generations.

Thus far, existing intergenerational programmes appear to be developed on a relatively small scale and somewhat piecemeal fashion, offered by various non-governmental and voluntary welfare organisations. Whilst these initiatives are commendable and should be encouraged, a more concerted and coordinated approach is proposed here. Educational institutions could systematically expand such programmes, by recruiting and deploying seniors to be mentors and equipping them to be para-/counsellors or guidance officers. The initial target groups could be youths-at-risk, and subsequently the programmes could be expanded to include other youths in general. However, the initial focus on youths-at-risk should be carried out with tact and sensitivity, to reduce stigmatisation. To enhance mutual appreciation and respect between the generations, youths could also be equipped with relevant skills to "reverse mentor" seniors, for example, in technological or other skills. This could enhance the self-esteem of youths, particularly at-risk youths, who may feel inadequate academically.

Yet another approach could be for students to be assigned to undertake a module or a semester working in partnership with an older adult. The organic relationship that might develop from such arrangements could have many protective layers for both the young and the old. The mental health of both the young and the elderly have been reported to be on the decline since the pandemic, due to loneliness and social isolation. Such intergenerational activities could have the potential to address some of the mentioned mental health challenges. Moreover, with the issue of ageism still rather pervasive in Singapore society, such intergenerational programmes and activities might contribute to the mitigation of negative stereotypes held by youths, such as older persons being perceived as "slow and senile". Moreover, such initiatives may engender in our youths positive perceptions, attitudes and values of respect, patience and empathy for others, including older adults.

In line with the three key thrusts of Contribution, Care and Connectedness for successful ageing, this chapter has proposed several concrete recommendations to achieve this goal. These proposals straddle multiple arenas: workplaces, healthcare systems, family caregiving and intergenerational integration. As the *Action Plan for Successful Ageing* (MOH, 2016a) is scheduled to be refreshed in 2022, this is an opportune time to evaluate and consider how the plan can be further enhanced. The hope is that the proposals set out in this chapter will contribute towards the enhancement of existing initiatives, as well as the development of further new, innovative and appropriate ones to achieve Singapore's goal of facilitating seniors to age successfully in the community.

Chapter 14

Moving Forward

"The test of a people is how it behaves towards the old. It is easy to love children. Even tyrants and dictators make a point of being fond of children. But the affection and care for the old, the incurable, the helpless are the true gold mines of a culture."

Abraham J. Heschel

This book has documented the impact and implications of population ageing in Singapore society. It has discussed, in considerable depth, a broad spectrum of issues: age-associated physical and psychological changes; illnesses and healthcare costs; social care and integration of seniors; seniors' employment and financial concerns; and an ageing workforce. Additionally, it has recommended several public policies for deliberation. Whilst acknowledging the myriad challenges of longevity, this book has also highlighted the plethora of opportunities and possibilities of mitigating their impact, such as by harnessing the strengths and potential of seniors, and by using technology to do so. The hope is that readers will *not* view population ageing negatively as a threat to society, but recognise the dividends that can accrue from it.

However, moving forward, it should be emphasised that reaping these dividends is contingent upon the fulfilment of the following caveats. Firstly, it requires a re-examination of our commonly-held Assumptions about seniors; secondly, it necessitates their successful Assimilation or integration into society; thirdly, it requires the proactive promotion of their Agency and, finally, it engenders continuous Advocacy efforts for seniors. These will be elaborated in the following section.

Assumptions

Firstly, every individual and young person, and older adults themselves, their families, employers, professionals working with seniors and policymakers, *etc*, should critically re-examine their paradigms, that is, their fundamental assumptions, perceptions and beliefs about seniors. Such an exercise should lead to a re-formulation of organisational and social policies and practices. Moreover, it should precipitate the development of more innovative policies, programmes and services/supports to optimise seniors' potential and facilitate ageing-in-place. Most significantly, it should be noted that seniors are an extremely heterogenous group, in terms of functional abilities, educational levels, social circumstances, interests etc.

In light of the research evidence and strategies considered and discussed in this book, ageist myths, biases and stereotypical views about seniors should be discarded and updated with accurate information and evidence. Moreover, against the backdrop of technological advancements, where the impact of many age-associated conditions can be mitigated, re-examining stereotypical attitudes is even more pertinent.

Assimilation

The ongoing rhetoric of the Singapore government has been on building a caring and inclusive society, where no one gets left behind. Seniors are an integral part of society, and each is as intrinsically worthy as any human being or other member of our society, even if some may be decrepit, depressed, dependent and/or demented. As a nation which espouses social inclusion as a key ideological tenet, it is incumbent upon us to design and develop appropriate structures, supports and a conducive environment to fully assimilate them into society. Since the challenges, concerns, issues and aspirations of our seniors are multi-faceted, multi-dimensional, straddling multiple ministries, a more holistic, multi-pronged, whole-of-government approach is required to assimilate them more fully into society. Moreover, in view of the huge demographic imperative to bring into sharper focus the array of issues at the policymaking stage, the time is ripe for a Ministry on Ageing Issues to be established. The proposed ministry should not merely be a coordinating body on ageing, but should critically analyse the current and future ageing-related issues, and take the lead in formulating a coherent, comprehensive and forward-looking national policy on ageing, working in concert with other ministries, agencies and civil society groups (Ko, 2021c).

Agency

Despite various age-associated diseases and/or decrements, the research suggests that older adults value being able to make their own decisions and exercise their own choices. Therefore, they should be accorded their rights to choose and not simply be acted upon. We must not assume that their physical and/or functional declines always imply cognitive deficits in making decisions, or the absence of the desire to do so. Such personal *agency*, that is, their capacity to act according to their own free will, akin to what we would accord to other adults, should be promoted as much as feasible, even as we seek to protect those seniors who are vulnerable and/or at risk.

Advocacy

To fully include and integrate seniors into our society, we need to proactively inform, educate and engage more individuals and relevant stakeholders at multiple levels (individual, organisational, community and societal) to advocate for seniors. The information, to be disseminated widely and on a continuous basis, should be supported by research and clinical evidence. Therefore, going forward, more research should be carried out, not merely on the treatment of diseases but also on prevention, and to focus on the development of seniors' potential, in order to enact effective strategies and solutions to optimise the latter.

The phenomenon of longevity is an *achievement* and not an *affliction* of Singapore society. Seniors have contributed significantly to nation-building in Singapore, and they are capable of continuing to contribute in numerous meaningful ways to society. Therefore, let us harness their strengths and abilities, and empower those who require support and assistance to rise above the vicissitudes of ageing, by equipping every individual with the requisite knowledge and skills to turn our "silver" resources into "gold". This requires the concerted effort of all, from every sector of society.

We must remember in the way we value, respect, honour and care for our seniors that we shall be treated thus when we ourselves grow old.

Appendix

Community Resources (Selected)

HEALTH AND SOCIAL SERVICES
Ministry of Social and Family Development (MSF)
Provides a directory of services, ranging from children to the elderly.
www.msf.gov.sg
MSF Consolidated Hotline: 1800-111-2222

Health Promotion Board
Provides useful information on various diseases and medical conditions, as well as educational materials.
www.hpb.gov.sg

Agency for Integrated Care
Provides an "E-Care Locator", a search engine which allows you to browse through a directory of social and healthcare service providers which provide residential and community-based services to meet the needs of patients, family members, caregivers and the general public.
www.aic.sg
www.aic.sg/care-services/e-care-locator

Health Hub
Provides a digitised platform for individual health data and other information on health management, including psychosocial support and caregiver training.
www.healthhub.sg

SG Enable
Provides centralised information and referral services, administers various eldercare and disability schemes and coordinates social services to strengthen the national support network for the frail elderly and persons with disabilities to pursue independent and dignified lives.
www.sgenable.sg

Dementia Sg
Provides education for caregivers on dementia care and support for People Living with Dementia.
www.dementia.org.sg

Trans Safe Centre
Provides mitigation and help to victims of family violence.
www.trans.org.sg

SAGE Counselling Centre Seniors Helpline
Provides information and referral to various services for the elderly, counselling to enhance the total well-being of the older persons and their caregivers, with a special focus on the psychological and social aspects of their health.
Tel: 1800 555 5555

Samaritans of Singapore
Provides counselling for anyone in crisis and persons with suicidal tendencies, thinking of suicide or affected by suicide.
Tel: 1-767 (24 hours)

Care Corner Counselling Hotline
Provides Mandarin counselling serviced by professional counsellors.
Tel: 1800 353 5800

Hospices and Community Hospitals
Provides services, comfort and support to end-of-life patients.

Singapore Hospice
Provides information on palliative care services for home, hospices and community hospitals.
www.singaporehospice.org.sg

My Legacy
Provides a list of 19 hospices with their contacts and websites; and other information on end-of-life planning. Includes an LPA-ACP tool for guidance in Lasting Power of Attorney (LPA) and Advance Care Plan (ACP) forms completion.
www.mylegacy.life.gov.sg

HCA Hospice
www.hca.org.sg

Assisi Hospice
www.assisihospice.org.sg

Dover Park Hospice
www.doverpark.org.sg

St Joseph's Home
www.stjh.org.sg

Ang Mo Ko – Thye Hua Kwan Hospital
www.amkh.com.sg

St Luke's Hospital
www.slh.org.sg

St Andrew's Community Hospital
www.sach.org.sg

JOB-RELATED RESOURCES
SkillsFuture
Provides Singaporeans with programmes and courses to develop their fullest potential in their skills and employability.
www.skillsfuture.gov.sg

My Career Future
Provides a listing of job openings.
www.mycareersfuture.gov.sg

e2i
Provides career guidance and job matching services for workers and employers seeking employment and employability solutions in Singapore.
www.e2i.com.sg

WSG Workforce Singapore
Provides suites of services and programmes for jobseekers and enterprises.
www.wsg.gov.sg
www.ssg-wsg.gov.sg

SELF-HELP GROUPS

Chinese Development Assistance Council
Provides programmes and assistance schemes to aid the less privileged in the Chinese community.
www.cdac.org.sg

Yayasan MENDAKI
Provides assistance to students and individuals of the Malay/Muslim community in training and education.
www.mendaki.org.sg

Singapore Indian Development Association
Provides support in education and assists families in need in the Indian community.
www.sinda.org.sg

Eurasian Association
Provides services for the community in three key areas: educational advancement, family support services and community development.
www.eurasians.sg

COMMUNITY DEVELOPMENT COUNCILS (CDCS)

Provides financial and employment assistance, as well as referral to support services. There are five CDCs in Singapore:

Central Singapore CDC
490 Lorong 6 Toa Payoh, #07-11, HDB Hub BizThree, S(310490)
www.cdc.gov.sg/centralsingapore
Tel: 67157500

North East CDC
1 Tampines Walk #04-31, Our Tampines Hub, S(528523)
www.cdc.gov.sg/northeast
Tel: 6424 4000

North West CDC
900 South Woodlands Drive, #06-01, Woodlands Civic Centre, S(730900)
www.cdc.gov.sg/northwest
Tel: 62485566

South East CDC
1 Engku Aman Turn, #03-02, S(408528)
www.cdc.gov.sg/southeast
Tel: 6432 1300

South West CDC
8 Jurong Town Hall Road #26-06, The JTC Summit, S(609434)
www.cdc.gov.sg/southwest
Tel: 6316 1616

References

CHAPTER 1

Bersin, J., & Chamorro-Premuzic, T. (26 September 2019). "The Case for Hiring Older Workers." *Harvard Business Review*. https://hbr.org/2019/09/the-case-for-hiring-older-workers

Chan, A., Ostbye, T., Malhotra, R., & Hu, A. J. (2012). *The Survey on Informal Caregiving*. https://www.msf.gov.sg/publications/Documents/Informal%20Caregiver%20Survey%20Summary%20Report%20(upload).pdf

International Labour Organization [ILO]. (2019). *Supporting longer working lives: Multistage approaches for decent and productive work*. https://www.ilo.org/wcmsp5/groups/public/---dgreports/---cabinet/documents/publication/wcms_713371.pdf

Kang, S. H., Tan, E. S., & Yap, M. T. (April 2013). *National Survey of Senior Citizens 2011*. https://www.msf.gov.sg/publications/Documents/National%20Survey%20of%20Senior%20Citizens%202011_Complete_amended_use%20this%20CH.pdf

Ko, H. (27 July 2021a). "Commentary: Heeding cries for help – getting to the heart of elderly suicides requires more than counselling." *CNA*. https://www.channelnewsasia.com/commentary/elderly-suicide-cries-help-helpline-support-2077891

Mehta, K. K. & Thang, L. L. (2017). "Experiences of Formal and Informal Caregivers of Older Persons in Singapore." *Journal of Cross-cultural Gerontology*, 32(3), 373–385. https://doi.org/10.1007/s10823-017-9329-1

Ministry of Culture, Community and Youth. (2019). *Recognising the importance of senior volunteerism and active seniors.* https://www.mccy.gov.sg/about-us/news-and-resources/speeches/2019/feb/recognising-the-importance-of-senior-volunteerism-and-active-seniors

Ministry of Health [MOH]. (2016a). *Action Plan for Successful Ageing.* https://www.moh.gov.sg/docs/librariesprovider3/action-plan/action-plan.pdf

Ministry of Health [MOH]. (2019). *The Burden of Disease in Singapore, 1990–2017: An overview of the Global Burden of Disease Study 2017 results.* https://www.moh.gov.sg/docs/librariesprovider5/default-document-library/gbd_2017_singapore_reportce6bb0b3ad1a49c19ee6ebadc1273b18.pdf

Ministry of Health [MOH]. (2020). *National Population Health Survey 2020.* https://www.moh.gov.sg/docs/librariesprovider5/default-document-library/nphs-2020-survey-report.pdf

Mui, R. (27 August 2018). "Young people in Singapore worry their parents do not save enough for retirement – with good reason: Survey." *The Straits Times.* https://www.straitstimes.com/business/economy/singapore-youths-worry-their-parents-are-not-saving-enough-for-retirement-with-good

Poh, J. (2 September 2019). "Who Are The Sandwich Generation And Why Are They Struggling?" *Income.* https://www.income.com.sg/blog/who-are-the-sandwich-generation

Rudnicka, E., Napierała, P., Podfigurna, A., Męczekalski, B., Smolarczyk, R., & Grymowicz, M. (2020). "The World Health Organization (WHO) approach to healthy ageing." *Maturitas*, 139, 6–11. https://doi.org/10.1016/j.maturitas.2020.05.018

Singapore. Department of Statistics. (2021a). *Census of Population 2020*. https://www.singstat.gov.sg/-/media/files/publications/cop2020/sr1/cop2020sr1.pdf

Singapore. Department of Statistics. (2021b). *Death and life expectancy*. https://www.singstat.gov.sg/find-data/search-by-theme/population/death-and-life-expectancy/latest-data

Singh, A., & Misra, N. (2009). "Loneliness, depression and sociability in old age." *Industrial Psychiatry Journal*, 18(1), 51–55. https://doi.org/10.4103/0972-6748.57861

Tan, T. (14 April 2020). "Abuse of vulnerable folk like the elderly and those with disabilities almost doubles in 3 years." *The Straits Times*. https://www.straitstimes.com/singapore/abuse-of-vulnerable-folk-like-elderly-and-those-with-disabilities-almost-doubles-in-3

United Nations. (2019). *World Population Ageing 2019: Highlights*. https://www.un.org/en/development/desa/population/publications/pdf/ageing/WorldPopulationAgeing2019-Highlights.pdf

CHAPTER 2

Franceschi, C., Garagnani, P., Morsiani, C., Conte, M., Santoro, A., Grignolio, A., Monti, D., Capri, M., & Salvioli, S. (2018). "The Continuum of Aging and Age-Related Diseases: Common Mechanisms but Different Rates." *Frontiers in Medicine*, 5, 61. https://doi.org/10.3389/fmed.2018.00061

Ministry of Health [MOH] (2022). *Principal Causes of Death*. https://www.moh.gov.sg/resources-statistics/singapore-health-facts/principal-causes-of-death

Ow Yong, L., & Koe, L. W. P. (2021). "War on Diabetes in Singapore: a policy analysis." *Health Research Policy and Systems*, 19, Article 15. https://doi.org/10.1186/s12961-021-00678-1

SingHealth (n.d.). *Diabetes in Singapore: Stats and Prevention Tips*. https://www.healthxchange.sg/diabetes/essential-guide-diabetes/diabetes-singapore-stats-prevention-tips

Wang, P., Abdin, E., Shafie, S., Chong, S. A., Vaingankar, J. A., & Subramaniam, M. (2019). "Estimation of Prevalence of Osteoporosis Using OSTA and Its Correlation with Sociodemographic Factors, Disability and Comorbidities." *International Journal of Environmental Research and Public Health*, 16(13), 2338. https://doi.org/10.3390/ijerph16132338

CHAPTER 3

Charles, S. T., & Carstensen, L. L. (2010). "Social and emotional aging." *Annual Review of Psychology*, 61, 383–409. https://doi.org/10.1146/annurev.psych.093008.100448

Krause, N. (2006). "Neighborhood deterioration, social skills, and social relationships in late life." *The International Journal of Aging and Human Development*, 62(3), 185–207. https://doi.org/10.2190/7pvl-3ya2-a3qc-9m0b

Pauwels, L., Chalavi, S., & Swinnen, S. P. (2018). "Aging and brain plasticity." *Aging*, 10(8), 1789–1790. https://doi.org/10.18632/aging.101514

CHAPTER 4

Bergen, G., Stevens, M. R., & Burns, E. R. (2016). "Falls and Fall Injuries Among Adults Aged ≥65 Years – United States, 2014." *Morbidity and Mortality Weekly Report*, 65(37), 993–998. http://dx.doi.org/10.15585/mmwr.mm6537a2

Subramaniam, M., Abdin, E., Sambasivam, R., Vaingankar, J. A., Picco, L., Pang, S., Seow, E., Chua, B. Y., Magadi, H., Mahendran, R., & Chong, S. A. (2016). "Prevalence of Depression among Older Adults – Results from the Well-being of the Singapore Elderly Study." *Annals of the Academy of Medicine, Singapore*, 45(4), 123–133. https://pubmed.ncbi.nlm.nih.gov/27292002/

Vaingankar, J. A., Chong, S. A., Abdin, E., Picco, L., Chua, B. Y., Shafie, S., Ong, H. L., Chang, S., Seow, E., Heng, D., Chiam, P. C., & Subramaniam, M. (2017). "Prevalence of frailty and its association with sociodemographic and clinical characteristics, and resource utilization in a population of Singaporean older adults." *Geriatrics & Gerontology International*, 17(10), 1,444–1,454. https://doi.org/10.1111/ggi.12891

CHAPTER 5

Haseltine, W. A. (2013). *Affordable excellence: The Singapore healthcare story*. Brookings Institution Press.

Kisling, L. A., & Das, J. M. (2021). *Prevention Strategies*. StatPearls Publishing.https://www.ncbi.nlm.nih.gov/books/NBK537222/

Ng, R., Sutradhar, R., Yao, Z., Wodchis, W. P., & Rosella, L. C. (2020). "Smoking, drinking, diet and physical activity-modifiable lifestyle risk factors and their associations with age to first chronic disease." *International Journal of Epidemiology*, 49(1), 113–130. https://doi.org/10.1093/ije/dyz078

Seow, B. Y. (28 January 2018). *Social mobility, ageing are Singapore's big challenges: Tharman*. Ministry of Finance. https://www.mof.gov.sg/news-publications/media-articles/social-mobility-ageing-are-singapore's-big-challenges-tharman

Subramaniam, M., Abdin, E., Vaingankar, J. A., Sambasivam, R., Seow, E., Picco, L., Chua, H. C., Mahendran, R., Ng, L. L., & Chong, S. A. (2019). "Successful ageing in Singapore: Prevalence and correlates from a national survey of older adults." *Singapore Medical Journal*, 60(1), 22–30. https://doi.org/10.11622/smedj.2018050

Wong, H. Z., Lim, W. Y., Ma, S. S., Chua, L. A., & Heng, D. M. (2015). "Health Screening Behaviour among Singaporeans." *Annals of the Academy of Medicine, Singapore*, 44(9), 326–334.

Wee, L. E., Koh, G. C. H., & Toh, Z. J. (October 2010). "Multi-disease health screening in an urban low-income setting: a community-based study." *Annals of the Academy of Medicine, Singapore*, 39(10), 750–757. https://pubmed.ncbi.nlm.nih.gov/21063634/

Yuen. S. (28 January 2018). "Finding a cure for rising costs in healthcare." *The Straits Times*. https://www.straitstimes.com/politics/singapolitics/finding-a-cure-for-rising-costs-in-healthcare

CHAPTER 6

Butler, R. N. (1963). "The Life Review: An Interpretation of Reminiscence in the Aged." *Psychiatry*, 26(1), 65–76. https://doi.org/10.1080/00332747.1963.11023339

Chan, A., Ostbye, T., Malhotra, R., & Hu, A. J. (2012). *The Survey on Informal Caregiving*. https://www.msf.gov.sg/publications/Documents/Informal%20Caregiver%20Survey%20Summary%20Report%20(upload).pdf

Chan, C. K. L., & Yau, M. K. (1 May 2010). "Death Preparation among the Ethnic Chinese Well-Elderly in Singapore: An Exploratory Study." *OMEGA – Journal of Death and Dying*, 60(3), 225–239. https://doi.org/10.2190/om.60.3.b

Chan, F. (18 February 2015). "PM Lee asks families to bond – with a little help from Government." *The Straits Times*. https://www.straitstimes.com/singapore/pm-lee-asks-families-to-bond-with-a-little-help-from-government

Detering, K. M., Hancock, A. D., Reade, M. C., & Silvester, W. (24 March 2010). "The impact of advance care planning on end of life care in elderly patients: randomised controlled trial." *The BMJ*, 340, Article c1345. https://doi.org/10.1136/bmj.c1345

Elangovan, N. (13 July 2019). "Most Singaporeans want a 'good death', but majority don't get their wish: Study." *TODAY Online*. https://www.todayonline.com/singapore/good-death-more-needed-end-life-care-singapore-ips-study

Finkelstein, E., Malhotra, C., & Yee, A. C. P. (2014). "Improving the end-of-life experience in Singapore: building capacity in palliative care education and research." *Annals of the Academy of Medicine, Singapore*, 43(1), 1–2. https://pubmed.ncbi.nlm.nih.gov/24557458/

Hebert, R. S., Schulz, R. S., Copeland, V. C., & Arnold, R. M. (1 January 2009). "Preparing Family Caregivers for Death and Bereavement. Insights from Caregivers of Terminally Ill Patients." *Journal of Pain and Symptom Management*, 37(1), 3–12. https://doi.org/10.1016/j.jpainsymman.2007.12.010

Hinshaw, D. B. (2002). "The Spiritual Needs of the Dying Patient." *Journal of the American College of Surgeons*, 195(4), 565–568. https://doi.org/10.1016/s1072-7515(02)01328-5

Jennings, L. A., Palimaru, A., Corona, M. G., Cagigas, X. E., Ramirez, K. D., Zhao, T., Hays, R. D., Wenger, N. S., & Reuben, D. B. (20 December 2016). "Patient and caregiver goals for dementia care." *Quality of Life Research*, 26(3), 685–693. https://doi.org/10.1007/s11136-016-1471-7

Ko, H. (27 July 2021a). "Commentary: Heeding cries for help – getting to the heart of elderly suicides requires more than counselling." *CNA*. https://www.channelnewsasia.com/commentary/elderly-suicide-cries-help-helpline-support-2077891

Kozlov, E., Phongtankuel, V., Prigerson, H., Adelman, R., Shalev, A., Czaja, S., Dignam, R., Baughn, R., & Reid, M. C. (17 April 2019). "Prevalence, Severity, and Correlates of Symptoms of Anxiety and Depression at the Very End of Life." *Journal of Pain and Symptom Management*, 58(1), 80–85. https://doi.org/10.1016/j.jpainsymman.2019.04.012

Kwok, T., Twinn, S., & Yan, E. (17 April 2007). "The attitudes of Chinese family caregivers of older people with dementia towards life sustaining treatments." *Journal of Advanced Nursing*, 58(3), 256–262. https://doi.org/10.1111/j.1365-2648.2007.04230.x

Lee, G. L., & Tan, C. Y. (2020). "Chapter 9: Social Work in Palliative and Hospice Care." In G. L. Lee & S. N. Goh (eds.). *Medical Social Work In Singapore: Context and Practice*. pp 169–188. World Scientific. https://doi.org/10.1142/9789811227493_0009

Malhotra, C., Koh, L. E., Teo, I., Ozdemir, S., Chaudhry, I., Finkelstein, E., & COMPASS Study Team (5 August 2021). "A Prospective Cohort Study of Stability in Preferred Place of Death Among Patients With Stage IV Cancer in Singapore." *Journal of the National Comprehensive Cancer Network*, 20(1). https://doi.org/10.6004/jnccn.2020.7795

Mehta, K. K. (2007). "Multigenerational relationships within the Asian family: Qualitative evidence from Singapore." *International Journal of Sociology of the Family*, 33(1), 63–77. http://www.jstor.org/stable/23070763

Morgan, L. A., & Kunkel, S. R. (2015). *Aging, Society, and the Life Course*. (5th Ed.). Springer Publishing Company. https://doi.org/10.1891/9780826121738

Phua, J., Kee, A. C.-L., Tan, A., Mukhopadhyay, A., See, K. C., Aung, N. W., Seah, A. S. T., & Lim, T. K. (6 December 2011). "End-of-Life Care in the General Wards of a Singaporean Hospital: An Asian Perspective." *Journal of Palliative Medicine*, 14(12), 1296–1301. https://doi.org/10.1089/jpm.2011.0215

Schulz, R., Mendelsohn, A. B., Haley, W. E., Mahoney, D., Allen, R. S., Zhang, S., Thompson, L., & Belle, S. H. (13 November 2003). "End-of-Life Care and the Effects of Bereavement on Family Caregivers of Persons with Dementia." *The New England Journal of Medicine*, 349(20), 1936–1942. https://doi.org/10.1056/nejmsa035373

Singapore Management University [SMU]. (5 October 2019). *SMU study shows Singaporeans are more comfortable discussing end-of-life matters*. https://news.smu.edu.sg/news/2019/10/05/smu-study-shows-singaporeans-are-more-comfortable-discussing-end-life-matters

CHAPTER 7

Cheow, S., & Goh, R. (25 July 2019). "Elder abuse cases more than doubled in two years: Social and Family Development Ministry." *The Straits Times*. https://www.straitstimes.com/singapore/elderly-abuse-cases-more-than-doubled-in-two-years-msf

Subramanian, S. V., Elwert, F., & Christakis, N. (2008). "Widowhood and mortality among the elderly: The modifying role of neighborhood concentration of widowed individuals." *Social Science & Medicine*, 66(4), 873–884. https://doi.org/10.1016/j.socscimed.2007.11.029

Samaritans of Singapore [SOS]. (2018). *Suicide rate lowest, but number of elderly suicide highest recorded.* https://www.sos.org.sg/pressroom/suicide-rate-lowest-but-number-of-elderly-suicide-highest-recorded

Walsh, K., King, M., Jones, L., Tookman, A., & Blizard, R. (29 June 2002). "Spiritual beliefs may affect outcome of bereavement: Prospective study." *The BMJ*, 324, 1551. https://doi.org/10.1136/bmj.324.7353.1551

Wong, J. C. M. (2018). "Predicting Suicide and its Prevention." *Annals of the Academy of Medicine, Singapore*, 47(9), 357–359. https://annals.edu.sg/pdf/47VolNo9Sep2018/MemberOnly/V47N9p357.pdf

Yon, Y., Mikton, C. R., Gassoumis, Z. D., & Wilber, K. H. (February 2017). "Elder abuse prevalence in community settings: a systematic review and meta-analysis." *The Lancet*, 5(2), Article e147–e156. https://doi.org/10.1016/S2214-109X(17)30006-2

CHAPTER 8

Agency for Integrated Care. (2018). "Integrated Home and Day Care (IHDC) programme." *SMA News*, 50(7), 26–27. https://www.sma.org.sg/UploadedImg/1615533759_Full%20PDF.pdf

Housing and Development Board [HDB]. (10 May 2021). *Community Care Apartments.* https://www.hdb.gov.sg/residential/buying-a-flat/finding-a-flat/types-of-flats/community-care-apartments

Kang, S. H., Tan, E. S., & Yap, M. T. (April 2013). *National Survey of Senior Citizens 2011.* https://www.msf.gov.sg/publications/Documents/National%20Survey%20of%20Senior%20Citizens%202011_Complete_amended_use%20this%20CH.pdf

Ministry of Health [MOH]. (2016a). *Action Plan for Successful Ageing.* https://www.moh.gov.sg/docs/librariesprovider3/action-plan/action-plan.pdf

Ministry of Social and Family Development [MSF]. (2019). *Families and households in Singapore, 2000–2017*. https://vdocuments.net/families-and-households-in-singapore-2000-2017-families-and-households-in-singapore.html?page=1

Yap, M. T. (2010). "The Ageing Population." In Terence Chong (ed.), *Management of Success: Singapore Revisited* (pp. 183–198). Institute of Southeast Asian Studies.

CHAPTER 9

Begum, S. (4 July 2021). "Seniors less receptive to telemedicine and uncomfortable with AI interpreting medical results: S'pore Survey." *The Straits Times*. https://www.straitstimes.com/singapore/health/seniors-less-receptive-to-telemedicine-and-uncomfortable-with-ai-interpreting

Caplan, S. E., Haslett, B. J., & Burleson, B. R. (2005). "Telling It Like It Is: The Adaptive Function of Narratives in Coping With Loss in Later Life." *Health Communication*, 17(3), 233–251. https://doi.org/10.1207/s15327027hc1703_2

Chaudhuri, S., Thompson, H., & Demiris, G. (2014). "Fall Detection Devices and Their Use With Older Adults: A Systematic Review." *Journal of Geriatric Physical Therapy*, 37(4), 178–196. https://doi.org/10.1519/JPT.0b013e3182abe779

De Miguel, K., Brunete, A., Hernando, M., & Gambao, E. (2017). "Home Camera-Based Fall Detection System for the Elderly." *Sensors*, 17(12), 2864. https://doi.org/10.3390/s17122864

Ekwaru, J. P., Ohinmaa, A., & Veugelers, P. J. (2015). "The effectiveness of a preventive health program and vitamin D status in improving health-related quality of life of older Canadians." *Quality of Life Research, 25(3)*, 661–668. https://doi.org/10.1007/s11136-015-1103-7

Fischer, S. H., David, D., Crotty, B. H., Dierks, M., & Safran, C. (2014). "Acceptance and use of health information technology by community-dwelling elders." *International Journal of Medical Informatics*, 83(9), 624–635. https://doi.org/10.1016/j.ijmedinf.2014.06.005

Foo, K., Merrick, P. L., & Kazantzis, N. (2006). "Counseling/Psychotherapy With Chinese Singaporean Clients." *Asian Journal of Counselling*, 13(2), 271–293.

Grimmer, M., Riener, R., Walsh, C. J., & Seyfarth, A. (2019). "Mobility related physical and functional losses due to aging and disease – a motivation for lower limb exoskeletons." *Journal of NeuroEngineering and Rehabilitation*, 16(1), Article 2. https://doi.org/10.1186/s12984-018-0458-8

Han, E., Shiraz, F., Haldane, V., Koh, J. J. K., Quek, R. Y. C., Ozdemir, S., Finkelstein, E. A., Jafar, T. H., Choong, H., Gan, S., Lim, L. W. W., & Legido-Quigley, H. (2019). "Biopsychosocial experiences and coping strategies of elderly ESRD patients: A qualitative study to inform the development of more holistic and person-centred health services in Singapore." *BMC Public Health*, 19(1), Article 1107. https://doi.org/10.1186/s12889-019-7433-6

Hemmatpour, M., Ferrero, R., Montrucchio, B., & Rebaudengo, M. (2019). "A Review on Fall Prediction and Prevention System for Personal Devices: Evaluation and Experimental Results." *Advances in Human-Computer Interaction*, 2019(1), 1–12, Article 9610567. https://doi.org/10.1155/2019/9610567

Hummel, J., Weisbrod, C., Boesch, L., Himpler, K., Hauer, K., Hautzinger, M., Gaebel, A., Zieschang, T., Fickelscherer, A., Diener, S., Dutzi, I., Krumm, B., Oster, P., & Kopf, D. (1 April 2017). "AIDE—Acute Illness and Depression in Elderly Patients. Cognitive Behavioral Group Psychotherapy in Geriatric Patients With Comorbid Depression: A Randomized, Controlled Trial." *Journal of the American Medical Directors Association*, 18(4), 341–349. https://doi.org/10.1016/j.jamda.2016.10.009

Igual, R., Medrano, C., & Plaza, I. (2013). "Challenges, issues and trends in fall detection systems." *BioMedical Engineering OnLine*, 12(1), Article 66. https://doi.org/10.1186/1475-925x-12-66

Kim, H., & Kim, J. (2020). "The effect of Preparation for Old Age on the Life Satisfaction of the Korean Elderly: Focusing on the interaction effect of Social Support and Death Anxiety." *The Journal of the Korea Contents Association*, 20(10), 449–457. https://doi.org/10.5392/JKCA.2020.20.10.449

Ko, H. (2020a). *Counselling Older Adults: An Asian Perspective*. (2nd Ed.). Write Editions.

Ko, H. (27 July 2021a). "Commentary: Heeding cries for help – getting to the heart of elderly suicides requires more than counselling." *CNA*. https://www.channelnewsasia.com/commentary/elderly-suicide-cries-help-helpline-support-2077891

Kong, L., & Woods, O. (2018). "Smart eldercare in Singapore: Negotiating agency and apathy at the margins." *Journal of Aging Studies*, 47(1), 1–9. http://doi.org/10.1016/j.jaging.2018.08.001

Lam, W. W. Y., Loo, B. P. Y., & Mahendran, R. (2020). "Neighbourhood environment and depressive symptoms among the elderly in Hong Kong and Singapore." *International Journal of Health Geographics*, 19, Article 48. https://doi.org/10.1186/s12942-020-00238-w

Lai, S. H. S, & Tang, C. Q. Y. (2020). "Telemedicine and COVID-19: Beyond just virtual consultations – the Singapore experience." *Bone & Joint Open*, 1(6), 203–204. https://doi.org/10.1302/2633-1462.16.BJO-2020-0042.R1

Lau, Y. W., Vaingankar, J. A., Abdin, E., Shafie, S., Jeyagurunathan, A., Zhang, Y., Magadi, H., Ng, L. L., Chong, S. A., & Subramaniam, M. (2019). "Social support network typologies and their association with dementia and depression among older adults in Singapore: A cross-sectional analysis." *BMJ Open*, 9(5), Article e025303. https://doi.org/10.1136/bmjopen-2018-025303

Lino, V. T. S., Portela, M. C., Camacho, L. A. B., Atie, S., & Lima, M. J. B. (2013). "Assessment of Social Support and Its Association to Depression, Self-Perceived Health and Chronic Diseases in Elderly Individuals Residing in an Area of Poverty and Social Vulnerability in Rio de Janeiro City, Brazil." *Plos One*, 8(8), Article 71712. https://doi.org/10.1371/journal.pone.0071712

Mahendran, R., Feng, L., Ng, T. P., & Kua, E. H. (2013). "Successful ageing in Singapore – a viable goal?" *Annals of the Academy of Medicine, Singapore*, 42(1), 5–6. https://pubmed.ncbi.nlm.nih.gov/23417585/

Malhotra, R., Bautista, M. A. C., Müller, A. M., Aw, S., Koh, G. C. H., Theng, Y., Hoskins, S. J., Wong, C. H., Miao, C., Lim, W., Malhotra, C., & Chan, A. (2019). "The Aging of a Young Nation: Population Aging in Singapore." *The Gerontologist*, 59(3), 401–410. https://doi.org/10.1093/geront/gny160

Mehta, K. K., & Ko, H. (2014). *Gerontological Counselling: An Introductory Handbook*. (2nd Ed.). Write Editions.

Ng, T. P., Broekman, B. F. P., Niti, M., Gwee, X., & Kua, E. H. (1 May 2009). "Determinants of Successful Aging Using a Multidimensional Definition Among Chinese Elderly in Singapore." *The American Journal of Geriatric Psychiatry*, 17(5), 407–416. https://doi.org/10.1097/JGP.0b013e31819a808e

Ng, C. W. M., How, C. H., & Ng, Y. P. (2016). "Major depression in primary care: Making the diagnosis." *Singapore Medical Journal*, 57(11), 591–597. https://doi.org/10.11622/smedj.2016174

Pang, I., Okubo, Y., Sturnieks, D., Lord, S. R., & Brodie, M. A. (January/March 2019). "Detection of Near Falls Using Wearable Devices: A Systematic Review." *Journal of Geriatric Physical Therapy*, 42(1), 48–56. https://doi.org/10.1519/JPT.0000000000000181

Rajagopalan, R., Litvan, I., & Jung, T. (2017). "Fall Prediction and Prevention Systems: Recent Trends, Challenges, and Future Research Directions." *Sensors*, 17(11), 2509. https://doi.org/10.3390/s17112509

Rozario, P. A., & Rosetti, A. L. (2012). "'Many Helping Hands': A review and analysis of long-term care policies, programs, and practices in Singapore." *Journal of Gerontological Social Work*, 55(7), 641–658. https://doi.org/10.1080/01634372.2012.667524

Tan, L. F., Teng, V. H. W., Seetharaman, S. K., & Yip, A. W. (2020). "Facilitating telehealth for older adults during the COVID-19 pandemic and beyond: Strategies from a Singapore geriatric center." *Geriatrics & Gerontology International*, 20(10), 993–995. https://doi.org/10.1111/ggi.14017

Tao, Y., Zhang, W., Gou, Z., Jiang, B., & Qi, Y. (2021). "Planning Walkable Neighborhoods for 'Aging in Place': Lessons from Five Aging-Friendly Districts in Singapore." *Sustainability*, 13(4), 1742. https://doi.org/10.3390/su13041742

CHAPTER 10

Baker, J. A. (29 August 2021). "NDR 2021: Singapore to enshrine into law workplace anti-discrimination guidelines." *CNA*. https://www.channelnewsasia.com/singapore/ndr-2021-anti-discrimination-law-tafep-pm-lee-2143101

Beers, H. (17–18 June 2014). *Age, employment and the health and safety of the workforce: Health and Safety Laboratory* [Conference Session]. Institution of Occupational Safety and Health (IOSH) Conference, Buxton, UK.

Choi, E., Ospina, J., Steger, M. F., & Orsi, R. (2018). "Understanding work enjoyment among older workers: The significance of flexible work options and age discrimination in the workplace." *Journal of Gerontological Social Work*, 61(8), 1–20. https://doi.org/10.1080/01634372.2018.1515140

Iau, J. (20 March 2020). "MOM penalises 5 employers for age discrimination in hiring practices." *The Straits Times*. https://www.straitstimes.com/singapore/manpower/mom-penalises-5-employers-for-age-discrimination-in-hiring-practices

International Labour Organisation [ILO]. (8 September 2021). *Getting older: confronting Asia and the Pacific's ageing labour force*. https://www.ilo.org/asia/media-centre/news/WCMS_818956/lang--en/index.htm

Johan, S., & Manap, N. (March 2021). Research Brief Series: 10 – *Triumphs and Tribulations of Older Workers: Findings from a focus group inquiry into work-related motivations, skills and challenges among older Singaporeans*. Centre for Ageing

Research and Education (CARE). https://www.duke-nus. edu.sg/docs/librariesprovider3/research-policy-brief-docs/ triumphs-and-tribulations-of-older-workers-findings-from-a-focus-group-inquiry-into---amended5342e88c41de4d129 81389305e25ea61.pdf?sfvrsn=a5ebdc19_0

Johnson, S. J., Holdsworth, L., Hoel, H., & Zapf, D. (14 March 2013). "Customer stressors in service organizations: The impact of age on stress management and burnout." *European Journal of Work and Organizational Psychology*, 22(3), 318–330. https://doi.org/10.1080/1359432X.2013.772581

Ko, H. (2 February 2021b). "Commentary: Seniors do well at their jobs yet ageist myths and negative stereotypes persist." *CNA*. https://www.channelnewsasia.com/commentary/retirement-re-employment-age-raised-cpf-withdrawal-65-68-70-867116

Krause, N., Brand, R. J., Arah, O. A., & Kauhanen, J. (2015). "Occupational physical activity and 20-year incidence of acute myocardial infarction: results from the Kuopio Ischemic Heart Disease Risk Factor Study." *Scandinavian Journal of Work, Environment & Health*, 41(2), 124–139. https://doi.org/10.5271/sjweh.3476

Manpower Research and Statistics Department [MRSD]. (2016). *Labour force in Singapore, 2016.*

Ministry of Manpower [MOM]. (1 August 2019). *Report of the Tripartite Workgroup on Older Workers: Strengthening support for older workers.* https://www.mom.gov.sg/-/media/mom/documents/press-releases/2019/0819-twg-ow-report.pdf

Ministry of Manpower [MOM]. (12 October 2020). *Responsible re-employment.* https://www.mom.gov.sg/employment-practices/re-employment

Ministry of Manpower [MOM]. (28 January 2021). *Labour Force in Singapore: Impact of COVID-19 on the Labour Market. 2020 edition.* https://stats.mom.gov.sg/iMAS_PdfLibrary/mrsd_2020LabourfForce.pdf

Ministry of Manpower [MOM]. (8 March 2022). *Expansion of Progressive Wage Approach and Coverage.* https://www.mom.gov.sg/employment-practices/progressive-wage-model/expansion-of-progressive-wage-approach-and-coverage#:~:text=The%20Government%20has%20accepted%20all,more%20local%20lower%2Dwage%20workers

Petersen, C. B., Eriksen, L., Tolstrup, J. S., Søgaard, K., Grønbaek, M., & Holtermann, A. (2012). "Occupational heavy lifting and risk of ischemic heart disease and all-cause mortality." *BMC Public Health*, 12, Article 1070. https://doi.org/10.1186/1471-2458-12-1070

Rahn, G., Martiny, S. E., & Nikitin, J. (2021). "Feeling Out of Place: Internalized Age Stereotypes Are Associated With Older Employees' Sense of Belonging and Social Motivation." *Work, Aging and Retirement*, 7(1), 61–77. https://doi.org/10.1093/workar/waaa005

Rowe, J. W., & Kahn, R. L. (10 July 1987). "Human Aging: Usual and successful." *Science*, 237(4811), 143–149. https://doi.org/10.1126/science.3299702

Tripartite Alliance for Fair and Progressive Employment Practices [TAFEP]. (May 2013). *The value of mature workers to organisations in Singapore.* https://www.tal.sg/tafep/-/media/TAL/Tafep/Employment-Practices/Files/The-value-of-mature-workers-to-organisations-in-Singapore_2014.pdf

United Nations, Economic and Social Commission for Asia and the Pacific [ESCAP]. (2017). *Economic and Social Survey of Asia and The Pacific 2017 – Governance and Fiscal Management.* https://www.unescap.org/sites/default/d8files/knowledge-products/Survey%202017-Final.pdf

CHAPTER 11

Billett, S., Lim, P., Seet, J. F., Soh, Y. C., Wong, N., Yeo, T., Ong, G., Koh, T. S., Choy, M., Lizaso, M., Tan, J., & Ang, J. (July 2010). *Promoting and supporting lifelong employability for Singapore's workers aged 45 and over.* Institute for Adult Learning.

Ko, H. (2018). "Holistic framework for harnessing an ageing workforce in Singapore." In A. Sakamoto & J. Sung (eds.). *Skills and the Future of Work: Strategies for Inclusive Growth in Asia and the Pacific* (pp 100–124). International Labour Organisation, Regional Office for Asia and the Pacific.

Ko, H. (2 February 2021b). "Commentary: Seniors do well at their jobs yet ageist myths and negative stereotypes persist." *CNA*. https://www.channelnewsasia.com/commentary/retirement-re-employment-age-raised-cpf-withdrawal-65-68-70-867116

Lou, V., Leung, V. W. Q., Cheng, C. Y. M., Li, D. K. F., & Leung, Y. H. Y. (2017). *Best practices of elderly employment: A qualitative enquiry of elderly-friendly employment practice*. Hong Kong, China, Sau Po Centre on Ageing, University of Hong Kong.

Morschhäuser, M., & Sochert, R. (2006). *Healthy Work in an Ageing Europe: Strategies and Instruments for Prolonging Working Life*. European Network for Workplace Health Promotion. http://www.ageingatwork.eu/resources/health-work-in-an-ageing-europe-enwhp-3.pdf

World Health Organisation [WHO]. (2020). *UN Decade of Healthy Ageing: 2021–2030*. https://www.who.int/ageing/decade-of-healthy-ageing

Yong, C. (22 April 2022). "Flexible work arrangements should be a permanent feature: Tripartite statement." *The Straits Times*. https://www.straitstimes.com/singapore/flexible-work-arrangements-should-be-a-permanent-feature-tripartite-statement

CHAPTER 12

Duay, D. L., & Bryan, V. C. (2008). "Learning in Later Life: What Seniors Want in a Learning Experience." *Educational Gerontology*, 34(12), 1070–1086. https://doi.org/10.1080/03601270802290177

Fuller, A., & Unwin, L. (2005). "Older and wiser?: workplace learning from the perspective of experienced employees." *International Journal of Lifelong Education*, 24(1), 21–39. https://doi.org/10.1080/026037042000317329

Goh, V., Maulod, A., & Malhotra, R. (March 2021). Research Brief Series: 9 – *The Pursuit of Learning among Older Singaporeans*. Centre for Ageing Research and Education (CARE). https://www.duke-nus.edu.sg/docs/librariesprovider3/publications-docs/the-pursuit-of-learning-among-older-singaporeans.pdf?sfvrsn=24a70113_0

Ko, H. (13 August 2020b). "Teaching older adults: an instructional model from Singapore." *Educational Gerontology*, 46(12), 731–745. https://doi.org/10.1080/03601277.2020.1807689

Lee, C. C., Czaja, S. J., & Sharit, J. (2008). "Training Older Workers for Technology-Based Employment." *Educational Gerontology*, 35(1), 15–31. https://doi.org/10.1080/03601270802300091

Ministry of Health [MOH]. (2016a). *Action Plan for Successful Ageing*. https://www.moh.gov.sg/docs/librariesprovider3/action-plan/action-plan.pdf

Ministry of Health [MOH]. (4 May 2016b). "Learn For Fun, Learn For Life" At The National Silver Academy [Press Release]. https://www.moh.gov.sg/news-highlights/details/learn-for-fun-learn-for-life-at-the-national-silver-academy

Narushima, M., Liu, J., & Diestelkamp, N. (2018). "Lifelong learning in active ageing discourse: its conserving effect on wellbeing, health and vulnerability." *Ageing and Society*, 38(4), 651–675. https://doi.org/10.1017/S0144686X16001136

Pillay, H. K., Kelly, K., & Tones, M. (26 January 2010). "Transitional employment aspirations for bridging retirement: Implications for training and development." *Journal of European Industrial Training*, 34(1), 70–86.

SkillsFuture Singapore. (13 November 2020). *Programmes and Initiatives*. https://www.ssg-wsg.gov.sg/programmes-and-initiatives.html

CHAPTER 13

Beamish, R., & Wolfe, S. (eds.). (June 2016). *Hidden in Plain Sight: How Intergenerational Relationships Can Transform Our Future*. Stanford Center on Longevity. https://longevity.stanford.edu/wp-content/uploads/sites/24/2018/09/Intergenerational-relationships-SCL.pdf

Hawley-Hague, H., Horne, M., Campbell, M., Demack, S., Skelton, D. A., & Todd, C. (2013). "Multiple Levels of Influence on Older Adults' Attendance and Adherence to Community Exercise Classes." *The Gerontologist*, 54(4), 599–610. https://doi.org/10.1093/geront/gnt075

Jordan-Marsh, M., & Harden, J. T. (2005). "Fictive Kin: Friends as Family Supporting Older Adults as They Age." *Journal of Gerontological Nursing*, 31(2), 24–59. https://doi.org/10.3928/0098-9134-20050201-07

Ko, H. (13 August 2020b). "Teaching older adults: an instructional model from Singapore." *Educational Gerontology*, 46(12), 731–745. https://doi.org/10.1080/03601277.2020.1807689

Ministry of Health [MOH]. (2016a). *Action Plan for Successful Ageing*. https://www.moh.gov.sg/docs/librariesprovider3/action-plan/action-plan.pdf

Stathi, A., Mckenna, J., & Fox, K. R. (2010). "Processes Associated with Participation and Adherence to a 12-month Exercise Programme for Adults Aged 70 and older." *Journal of Health Psychology*, 15(6), 838–847. https://doi.org/10.1177/1359105309357090

CHAPTER 14

Ko, H. (2 February 2021c). "Commentary: It is high time for a Ministry on Ageing Issues." *CNA*. https://www.channelnewsasia.com/commentary/ageing-issues-ministry-singapore-policy-elderly-seniors-ageing-863041

Contributors

Celestine Wee is a nursing lecturer at the Alice Lee Centre for Nursing Studies, Yong Loo Lin School of Medicine, National University of Singapore. She graduated with a Master of Gerontology at the Singapore University of Social Sciences in 2020. With a keen interest in Gerontology, Celestine is passionate about equipping the next generation of nurses to meet the demands of an ageing population.

Dr Moses Ko graduated from the inaugural class of 2018 from the Lee Kong Chian School of Medicine, a partnership between Nanyang Technological University, Singapore, and Imperial College London. He was awarded the Toh Kian Chui Gold Medal for being the top performing student during the MBBS examinations. In recognition of his academic performance, leadership ability and contributions to society, he was also presented the Koh Boon Hwee Scholars Award. He is currently undergoing his specialist training to be a Family Physician.

Acknowledgements

This book would not have been possible without the assistance of my former Master of Gerontology students, Celestine Wee (who contributed Chapter 2) and Amy Lim (who helped to confirm the references and collated the community resources in the Appendix). I am very thankful for their help and contribution. As an educator, it is particularly gratifying for me to witness the professional growth and development of Celestine, and especially in her current role as a nursing lecturer at the Yong Loo Lin School of Medicine.

I greatly appreciate my son, Moses, for authoring Chapters 3 and 4. He is currently undergoing his specialist training to be a Family Physician. I am also extremely thankful for the support and encouragement of all my family members, throughout the writing process.

Finally, I am most grateful to God, for His countless blessings: education, counselling and teaching opportunities, as well as for very caring and supportive friends, bosses, colleagues and students. I have learned much from all of them, too. Special thanks to Professor Cheong Hee Kiat, for contributing to the Foreword of this book, as well as to Emeritus Professor Tsui Kai Chong and Associate Professor Lim Lee Ching for their unwavering support.

Without all of the above, it would not have been possible to pen this book.

About the Author

Dr Helen Ko is an Associate Professor with the Singapore University of Social Sciences, teaching courses in the in the Master and PhD in Gerontology and Master of Counselling programmes.

For over 30 years, A/Prof Ko pioneered the development of several programmes for seniors in Singapore: gerontological counselling, day care, case management services and seniors' employment/employability programmes. She had previously held key appointments as executive director/chief executive officer of various non-profit organisations, such as St Luke's Eldercare and Centre For Seniors.

A/Prof Ko has authored and co-authored five books, including a national bestseller, *Counselling Older Adults: An Asian Perspective* (Write Editions, 2nd Ed, 2020). Besides an indigenous model for counselling seniors, she has developed a model for teaching older adults, based on her award-winning research. She has also received the Singapore University of Social Sciences' Award for Teaching Excellence.

A/Prof Ko has served on various national committees in Singapore, including the Inter-Ministerial Committee on Ageing Population. She had previously served as Research Advisor for the Ministry of Social and Family Development and Board Director for the Council for Third Age and St Luke's Hospital. She is currently an Advisor for St Luke's Eldercare, and an Honorary Fellow of the University of Hong Kong's Sau Po Centre on Ageing.